John Ray (1627-1705)

Pioneer in the Natural Sciences

A Celebration and Appreciation of his life and work

Malcolm Bryan

Published by
The John Ray Trust
2005
The Town Hall Centre
Market Square
Braintree
Essex
CM7 3YG

Malcolm Bryan asserts the right to be identified as the author of this work.
Copyright 2005.

ISBN : 0-9550150-0-6

All rights reserved. No part of this publication may be reproduced, stored in a retrieval system, or transmitted, in any form or by any means, electronic, mechanical, photocopying, recording or otherwise, without the prior permission of the publishers.

Printed by
Banjo Printers and Stationers,
11 Perry Road,
Witham,
Essex. CM8 3YZ.

Cover design and artwork by Janet Turner
Front Cover illustrations: Meadow Buttercup, Purple Emperor Butterfly, Lesser Stag Beetle, Robin Redbreast, Burnished Brass Moth.
Back Cover: John Ray, from an oil painting by Mary Beale. White Admiral Butterfly.

The John Ray Trust

The John Ray Trust was established in 1986 to advance public awareness of the work and life of John Ray and to provide annual Bursaries for students and others undertaking short term projects in the natural sciences. A Scholarship scheme is also available, sponsored by a local company.

A Bronze statue of John Ray by Faith Winter is situated near the entrance to the Braintree District Museum. The museum includes the John Ray Room dedicated to his life and work. Details of the John Ray Walk are available at the museum or from the Trust's education officer.

Further details of the work of the Trust can be obtained from:

The Education Officer
The John Ray Trust
Town Hall Centre
Market Square
Braintree
Essex
CM7 3YG

Dedication

To my grandchildren. May their lives be filled with the love of nature, its abiding beauty and all its wonders.

Contents

Aims and Acknowledgements — page 5

Introduction — page 8

Part One: Life and Times — page 9

Part Two: Predecessors in the Natural Sciences — page 31

Part Three: John Ray's Contribution to the Natural Sciences — page 37

Part Four: Theology and Science — page 50

Part five: The Seventeenth Century — page 58

Part Six: John Ray's Legacy — page 71

Glossary — page 75

Biographical Details — page 78

Chronology — page 90

Sources — page 96

Aims and Acknowledgements

This book has been written for the general reader and all those interested in the natural world. My purpose is to bring to wider public attention the genius of John Ray, one of the most significant pioneers in the development of the natural sciences, a man of towering intellect and achievement, who lived over three hundred years ago.

In celebrating the tercentenary of his death it is appropriate that a new book is forthcoming, in particular to place him in the context of his predecessors and contemporaries and to appreciate the unique contribution he made.

His definitive Biographer in more recent times was Charles Raven, *John Ray Naturalist His Life and Works,* originally published in 1942. This mine of biographical information was reissued in 1986 in the Cambridge Science Classics Series to commemorate the 300 years since the Publication of the first volume of his most famous work *Historia Plantarum* (1686). Also in 1986 Stuart Baldwin wrote an informative booklet as his contribution to the celebrations of the time that also saw the setting up of the John Ray Trust.

As the present author I became Chairman of the Trust at its inaugural meeting in March 1986. Over the past nineteen years I have become increasingly interested in and intrigued by John Ray to the extent that I have given many talks to interested groups and organisations. This has led me to gather a considerable amount of information about John Ray's life and times. For a number of years I have wanted to include this information in a book that looked at his achievements as a man within his times.

I am neither a scientist nor an academic. I therefore claim no expertise other than that of a layman fascinated by the subject and wanting to share my admiration of his achievements with a wider public in keeping with the objectives of the John Ray Trust.

My principal sources, over the years and now, have been Charles Raven and Stuart Baldwin; Raven containing a monumental volume of material and references, Baldwin providing a more concise but excellent summary of Ray's achievements. My task, in this book, has been to re-present and re-order much of this material for the benefit of today's general reader. However, I have added material from numerous other sources and have listed them at the back of this book. Occasionally I have added my own observations, interpretations and conclusions.

None of this would have happened but for the persistence and initiative of Valerie Carpenter, then a Braintree District Councillor, who, some twenty years ago, took responsibility for bringing his fame back into public view. She persuaded the Chief Executive of the Council, Charles Daybell to set up a steering group to provide for a celebration of the 300th anniversary of the Publication of *Historia Plantarum*.

Charles Daybell was the catalyst for providing the membership of this steering group, of which I was an invited member. He then put a great deal of effort into ensuring that the proposal to establish a Charitable Trust was successful. The Trust, which held its first meeting in March 1986, was set up to promote awareness of John Ray's life and work and provide Bursaries for those working in the natural sciences.

Charles Daybell was also responsible for successful and significant fundraising exercises that provided both the initial capital for the Bursary fund and for the substantial statue of John Ray that stands in front of Braintree District Museum. The Museum additionally houses the John Ray Room dedicated to explaining his life and work.

Early in 2004 Dr Max Walters, who had written the introduction to the 1986 re-issuing of Raven's book, was seeking to ensure that the study of Ray's work was brought up to date and he kindly felt that I might be able to make a contribution to this task. His initiative became the catalyst for putting into action my long held desire to write a book on

John Ray. However a larger more extensive book is required to do justice to Max Walter's request and from an eminent natural scientist of the present times.

To all three, Valerie Carpenter, Charles Daybell and Max Walters, my thanks, for getting me involved and motivated.

My thanks to Bob Vickers for the illustrations he donated to the trust and which appear in this book. My special thanks also to Janet Turner, the Trust's education officer, for her help and support with this project, her assistance with proof reading and in helping prepare the work for publication.

My thanks also to Angela Tanner who assisted with the proof reading and who, together with her husband Alex, provided encouragement and support. My special thanks to my wife, Teresa, for her patience, tolerance and support over the many months when this book was being researched and written as well as for her help with proof reading. Finally my thanks to the Trustees and members of the Trust's Executive committee for their support and encouragement with this project.

This book, therefore, provides an introduction for those who do not know John Ray and further information for those who wish to know more about his life and times. I am confident that they will not fail to be amazed at his achievements.

Malcolm Bryan
March 2005

Introduction

John Ray died three hundred years ago. This book has been written at the tercentenary of his death to celebrate his achievements in the natural sciences and as an appreciation of the significant role he played in their advancement. My use of the term Pioneer in the title is deliberate, as my contention is that his principal role and achievement was in facilitating the significant development of the natural sciences.

He was born in November 1627 at Black Notley, still today a small rural village in northern Essex. He was to become the leading British natural scientist of the seventeenth century, substantially taking forward the work of his predecessors, providing inspiration and motivation for his contemporaries and those who have followed him.

He lived through challenging times relating to the practice of religion, the advancement of science and the battle for political power. This included the bitter civil war resulting in the execution of King Charles I, the decade of rule by Oliver Cromwell followed by the restoration of Charles II.

As we shall see, these events and changes not only provided the background to John Ray's life but also were to have major influences on the direction of his life's work.

His own religious beliefs were central to the way he conducted his life and approached his work leaving us with an awesome model of integrity, intellectual ability and industriousness. This is his story.

Part One
Life and Times

Early years and Influences

John Ray entered the world on the 29th November 1627, the third child of Roger and Elizabeth Ray. His brother, Roger, was three years older and his sister, Elizabeth, two. His parents undoubtedly provided him with values that became his own.

His love of nature developed as he accompanied his mother, a local herbalist, as she collected plants for her work. As they walked together in the countryside she would describe to him the types of plants that were of medicinal value for those who sought her assistance in treating a variety of health problems. Her deeply held religious views would also have formed an integral part of her conversation.

As a young boy John took a delight in the countryside which he later described as follows:

"First I was fascinated and then absorbed by the rich spectacle of the meadows in springtime: then I was filled with wonder and delight by the marvellous shape, colour and structure of the individual plants. I came to see the natural world as the glory of God made manifest in his creation"

John's father was a local blacksmith and therefore a skilled craftsman. John spent many hours watching him at his work. Here he learnt the importance of and relationship between the structure and function of those wooden and metal objects made and forged by his father. John later applied this understanding to his work in the natural sciences by identifying structural characteristics as the determining feature in differentiating between species.

As a child of five John had to cope with the death of his older brother, Roger, then aged eight, from smallpox. It has been suggested that this tragic family event contributed to John's lifelong caution in expressing his feelings, as well as confirming for him the primacy of human relationships over personal ambition.

Education

In his tenth year, in 1637, John commenced his formal education in what is now the Jesus Chapel of St Michael's Church, Braintree, about two miles from his home. The school had been in existence in the church for about a hundred years and was known as the Grammar School.

Each day he would walk through the countryside, along the track, over Hoppit Bridge and up the steep hill to St Michael's. There he was educated until the age of sixteen. The headmaster at the school was a Mr Love who soon discovered he had a pupil of unique distinction. The education John received revealed and trained his prodigious memory, methodical and orderly approach to his work and his delight in mathematics and languages. His handwriting was of a high standard and legible to the end of his life.

During John's formative years the succeeding two rectors at Black Notley church, situated within sight and just a few hundred yards from his home, were both former Cambridge University men. Thomas Goad and Joseph Plume would have known his parents given Roger Ray's work as Blacksmith and Elizabeth's skills as a provider of herbal remedies. Both would have recognised that John was a highly intelligent boy and it is probable that both they and the Headmaster, Mr Love, spoke to the rector of St Michael's about John's future.

The Rector of St Michael's at the time was Samuel Collins who had also been educated at Cambridge. Collins had encouraged the setting up of a number of charities and, at the time John was sixteen, he was in possession of a Scholarship for "worthy Scholars" to study at Catherine Hall, Cambridge. Thomas Hobbs, a wealthy businessman with local connections, had given this bequest.

Although Collins had previously been arranging for John to enter Trinity College, where he himself had studied, it was Catherine Hall where John began his undergraduate studies at the age of sixteen and a half.

Life and times at Cambridge

One can imagine the change brought about in his life by his having to leave his home to live in Cambridge. He was a young man used to a rural lifestyle. His separation from his parents and sister must have been difficult for him made tolerable by the challenge and excitement of his studies and the conviviality of new friends.

However, John remained at Catherine Hall for less than two years before transferring to Trinity College. His reasons for making the transfer were probably related to the death of his tutor, Daniel Duckfield, who died in 1645 and John's dislike of the teaching method that was by means of disputation. He much preferred the "politer arts and sciences" found at Trinity.

It was during his studies at Cambridge that the true extent of his ability was revealed. John's Tutor, Duport, also taught Isaac Newton, but assessed John to be a better pupil along with Isaac Barrow, "None of the rest comparable." John developed great skill in Greek, Latin and Hebrew, graduating with a B.A in 1647/48 and becoming a minor fellow at Trinity in 1649. After a further two years he became a Major Fellow after which he became a lecturer in Greek (1651), Mathematics (1653) and then reader in Humanities in 1655.

John's personality combined a level of personal charm with an amiable disposition. These traits were to help him get on well with his colleagues and made him sought after and valued as a tutor. He also became renowned for his speaking and preaching skills especially on the subject of Divinity.

While he was at Trinity his father died in 1656 and his growing financial independence enabled him to build a new home for his mother in Black Notley, which was named Dewlands.

However some four or five years before this, while in his early twenties, he became ill, possibly due to overwork. This resulted in a prolonged period of convalescence. As he later explained:

"I had become ill…and had to rest from more serious study." He started to take walks in the Cambridge countryside: "There was leisure to contemplate…. What lay constantly before the eyes and… so often trodden thoughtlessly underfoot, the various beauty of plants, the cunning craftsmanship of nature."

During these walks he began to consider a project that would lead him towards his life's work in the natural sciences. He decided to produce a catalogue of Cambridge plants that was to become one of the first books of local flora to be published (*Catalogus Plantarum circa Cantibrigium Nascentium.* 1660).

The walks through the Cambridge Countryside re-introduced him to the world of plants that had so fascinated him as a child. He struggled in vain to find anyone knowledgeable about plants at the university and decided that he must take upon himself the responsibility for the advancement of botany. He felt such work would be of advantage to the university as well as providing him with a great deal of pleasure.

His own words convey the sense of his excitement at the challenge:

"First of all I had to become familiar with all the literature, to compare the plants I found with the pictures, and when there seemed to be a resemblance to go fully into the descriptions. Gaining skill by experience I enquired of any unknown plant to what tribe and family it belonged or could be assigned. This taught me to notice points of similarity and saved a vast deal of labour. Then the desire arose to help others in their difficulties. I was eager to make progress myself. I wanted to entice my friends to share my pursuits. So the idea of the catalogue was formed."

Here at this point in his life, in his mid twenties, he could not have realised where this journey would take him. What had become a rekindled interest, then a pleasurable pastime away from his teaching duties, would become, in time, his all consuming exploration of the natural world.

Another important milestone was the friendship he developed with Francis Willughby, one of his students. Francis became one of his assistants in the production of the Cambridge Catalogue. Francis Willughby had come up to Cambridge in 1653, the only son of Sir Francis Willughby of Middleton Hall in Warwickshire. Francis embodied a handsome appearance, vivacious personality combining great enthusiasm, ability and industriousness. John was later to describe Francis as the person who was the catalyst for their decision and determination to encompass and place in some ordered system of classification all that existed in the natural world.

The significance of the Cambridge Catalogue

Before we return to the partnership between John and Francis it is instructive to return to the significance of the work John was undertaking on the Cambridge Catalogue. For it is in the way he went about his work that he began to reveal those special qualities which made him so significant in the development of the natural sciences.

In the Catalogue he explained his method of working and the rules he applied. He described how, wherever possible, he used the names taken from the works of his predecessors, Jean and Gaspard Bauhin, John Gerard and John Parkinson who was Botanist to Charles 1.

If earlier descriptions were not clear he used a collection of descriptive synonyms, each followed by an abbreviation of the author's name. Where a species had not been described before or where there was confusion or doubt he added from his own observations, accurately described details about the form of the plant (Morphology), habit, whether annual or perennial, time of flowering and medicinal uses.

He also provided the English names with their Latin equivalents in the index. His extensive knowledge of and expertise in Latin meant that his understanding of the Latin names given to plants was both comprehensive and accurate and these explanations were included in the catalogue. Finally he provided a three-page outline of classification derived from Jean Bauhin's *Historica Universalis Plantarum*, the only one available at the time.

One of John Ray's greatest contributions was in his methodical sorting and ordering of plants where previously there was much duplication and obscure description. He fully realised that before any credible attempt could be made at the classification of plants it was necessary to provide an accurate identification of each plant leading to confirmation of its species name and description.

In this way he was setting new standards in descriptive botany and laying the foundations of scientific botany, understanding of plant distribution and geography. This was a significant departure from the works of previous authors wherein featured much Astrology, Alchemy (the medical forerunner of chemistry) and superstition. In consequence John Ray's first book was not only important for botany but can rightly take its place in the history of science exemplifying the concept of scientific investigation, based on observation, experimentation and the analysis of facts set out by Bacon in his *Novum Organum, 1620.*

Charles Raven, in his definitive and detailed biography of John Ray, *(John Ray- Naturalist His Life and Works. 1942)* stated that "The knowledge that he gained from the Flora of Cambridgeshire would have been remarkable if he had possessed the books and collections of a modern student."

Given the developments in communication and information technology since Raven was writing, over sixty years ago, we can only heartily endorse his observations and pay tribute to John Ray's energy, methodical approach and powers of observation; an aspect of his undeniable genius in the development of the natural sciences.

Such was the level of his scholarship, some two hundred years later the Babington Flora of Cambridgeshire (1860) listed some 950 species, 700 of which had been recorded by John Ray. John's work on the Cambridge Catalogue included six years of collecting, often in the company of Francis Willughby and other friends, followed by three years preparing his notes for publication.

As we come to the year of the Publication of the Cambridge Catalogue (1660) major changes in the world about him were about to accelerate his determination to develop his understanding of the natural world.

Unpredictable Times - Ordination and Resignation

The university had been affected by those swirling events that led to the Civil War and the downfall of Charles I, in 1649, when John was aged twenty-one and still a minor fellow at Trinity.

The nature of the struggle between Royalists and Parliamentarians, that later in the century would lead to the first constitutional monarch (William III), had a number of consequences for Cambridge not least of which was to create political divisions within the university. This meant that those who wished to remain had to plough a careful furrow of tact and diplomacy.

In addition to the high regard with which John was held at Cambridge his preference had always been for a quiet unobtrusive lifestyle where he could be left to get on with his work and say his prayers in private or in the Chapel. Raven has asserted that John was a Puritan by belief, disdaining unnecessary ritual, in no way assertive about his religious practice and would have preferred to have avoided ordination, which was a college requirement. As John explained:

"I abhorred the imposition of any form of oath where refusal would lead to loss of office. I regarded such threats as immoral because I believe that the right to minister as a clergyman must be a matter of conviction and fitness"

He should have been ordained at the age of 22 in 1650 but because of the civil upheavals of the time Cambridge had relaxed the requirement "Since Bishops are abolished no person can be legally ordained and therefore the penalty of expulsion is void"

However the requirement was reinstated in 1658. It appears that this caused John to weigh up carefully the consequences of his wish not to be ordained against the advantages of remaining at Cambridge which he loved and his need to continue providing for his widowed mother. He therefore, if somewhat reluctantly, agreed to ordination, which took place on The 23rd December 1660 when he was, aged 33.

We will return to look in more detail at his beliefs and allegiances in parts four and five.

Eleven years of Travel

His Ordination in 1660 came in the year when he and his friends had begun an eleven-year period of travel as part of a grand project that both he and Francis Willughby had conceived, of making a systematic record of the natural world.

They had decided that it was important to make their observations in the locations where species were located. They could then be described and drawn in their natural setting. This required a considerable amount of walking and riding on horseback. At the time of their journeys there was little in the way of maps, cartography being in its early development. Compared to today one can only marvel at their determination in travelling long distances given the slow nature of any progress either by foot or horse.

It is interesting to imagine John and his companions as they made their way to the many distant places they travelled to in their quest to advance the study of nature. In

later years he would reflect on this decade of travel with pleasure and satisfaction:
"Mainly of happy memory and with the conviviality of good friends"
In this eleven year period when he was between 30 and 41 years of age (1658 – 1669) his recorded travels are as follows:

1658 – Norhampton, Warwickshire, Peak District, Manchester,
North Wales, Anglesey, Worcester, Cambridge
1660 – North East England and the Isle if Man
1661 – York, Glasgow and Carlisle
1662 – Sussex, London , Cambridge, North Wales, Gloucester,
Somerset, Devon, Cornwall, Sussex
1663 – Kent, Calais and the Rhine
1664 – Padua, Genoa, Naples, Sicily, Malta
1665 – Venice, Switzerland including Geneva
1666 – Paris, Calais and Essex
1667 – Cornwall, Dorset and Hampshire
1668 – Westmoreland and Yorkshire
1669 – Chester, Oxford and Dartford

These journeys were to provide him with a decade of detailed notes and drawings that, in later years, were the foundation of his botanical writing. They also helped to enlarge his understanding and study of different dialects and provided material for his book on Proverbs.

Crisis and opportunity
However it was in the early years of this decade, in 1662, that calamity was to strike, as far as his life and work at Cambridge was concerned. He had been Ordained two years when a crisis of conscience led him to resign from his position at Cambridge and cast himself adrift without income and unable to practice either as a tutor or clergyman.

Following the restoration of the monarchy Charles II, through the Act of Uniformity required all those holding public office and clergymen to swear an oath disavowing the Covenant. In effect this meant swearing that previously sworn allegiance to the Covenant was an unlawful Oath.

Charles had signed the covenant in 1650 while in Scotland. The Scots, who opposed episcopal hierarchy, wanting no bishops, had drawn up the Covenant in 1638. When Charles I ignored their wishes they set up a full Presbyterian system in Scotland.

Following the restoration of the monarchy Charles II went back on his oath, and brought in the Act of Uniformity. This contained the enactment: that before St Barthomelew's day in 1662 all Clergymen and, in the Universities, all who bore any office must make a solemn declaration to this effect:

'*There lies no obligation upon me, or any other person, from the oath* (i.e. the oath swearing allegiance to the Covenant)... *and the same was in itself an unlawful oath*'

Although John had not sworn such an oath he did not feel he could sign the document as it affronted his conscience and beliefs. In consequence on the 24th August 1662, at the age of 34, he found himself debarred from work both as a tutor and clergyman.

A Helping hand

At this bleak point in his life, where it appeared he had lost all he had been working for, his friend Francis Willughy came to his aid, effectively providing the financial support for John to continue with their travels as part of their grand project.

William Derham, in his life of Ray published in 1760 graphically described their mission:

"These two gentlemen, finding the 'history of Nature' very imperfect had agreed between themselves, before their

travels beyond the sea, to reduce the several tribes of things to a method: and to give accurate descriptions of the several species, from a strict view of them."
They set out therefore with a determination to record all that they could observe of both Flora and Fauna. (Plants, birds, animals, fishes and insects).

As has been mentioned previously, cartography was still in its infancy and they would have had to rely on two maps of England and Wales by Tudor cartographers, published in 1573 and 1579 which were the first detailed maps of the two kingdoms, the latter indicating rivers, towns and villages with conical figures representing hills. However no roads were identified and to progress from one place to another they would have had to ask local inhabitants.

Despite an Act of Parliament in 1555 that made the upkeep of roads a parish responsibility they were mostly in a poor state; dusty in summer and their deep ruts and holes becoming "ponds of liquid dirt" in winter, dangerous to those on foot as well as horsemen. From the vantagepoint of the early years of the twenty-first century such undertakings by John and Francis seem both heroic and awesome in scale. How could they not be concerned for their wellbeing and safety in such circumstances beset by such major travelling difficulties?

The first major publication from this exploration was John Ray's *Catalogus Plantarum Angliae et Insularum Adjacentium* (1670) dedicated to Willughby. In this publication and its supplement John stated that he had explored the country from Land's End in Cornwall to Berwick and Carlisle in the north, in order to see for himself the plants in their habitat.

John followed this with his *Synopsis Methodica Stirpium Britannicarum* (1690). Richard Pulteney stated in 1790 that this had been " the pocket companion of every English botanist."
When Linnaeus wrote his *Species Plantarum* (1753) his herbarium contained no British plants, his knowledge of

them coming from published works the most important being that of John Ray.

Returning to the period immediately following John's resignation, Francis Willughby had suggested a continental tour to extend their biological studies. On April 18th 1663 Willughby, Ray and two other colleagues sailed from Dover to Calais to begin a three-year tour that was probably one of the highlights of John's life. The primary purpose of the tour was to advance their knowledge of plants and animals. Ray also carried out a significant amount of work on Zoology. They studied birds and fishes in the markets and ports. In addition to the collecting of specimens John had the opportunity of meeting and conversing with other scientists, visiting their universities and studying their library collections. There can be little doubt that he was stimulated by these experiences which broadened his scientific understanding and cultural outlook.

John's busy eleven years of travelling or when back in England, working with Francis Willughby on their notes and collections, at Middleton Hall, Warwickshire, was soon to come to a tragic end.

An unexpected tragedy

In the summer of 1672 when John was proposing a further botanical expedition, Francis Willughby became ill and died on the 3rd July.

Francis's death at the early age of 37 effectively put an end to John's period of travel. Ironically it became the catalyst for the rest of his life's work, the writing and publishing of over thirty books that were to establish his reputation as the greatest natural historian of the seventeenth century. Later, as one of the two principal purposes of this book, John's specific achievements in the natural sciences will be described, illustrating his unique contribution with an appreciation of his work set against the background of those who had preceded him.

Raven, in his biography of Ray, stated his opinion that the death of Francis Willughby was a more serious blow to John than the loss of his fellowship at Cambridge. It was almost certainly keenly felt. The sudden nature of Francis's death and the depth of their relationship had encompassed a professional partnership that spanned the decade since John's resignation, based on their ambitious plans relating to the study of the natural world. Raven argued that the significance of their professional relationship and friendship was borne out by John's determination not to abandon their joint project and in the energy with which he took up the task of caring for the education of Willughby's children.

In his Will Francis Willughby granted John an annuity of £60 for life and for the next three and a half years Middleton Hall became his home. Francis' widow, Emma, seems to have had little regard for John and he remained there probably more because of the high esteem he was held in by Francis' elderly mother, Lady Cassandra and his concern for the education of the children. It was also a suitable and comfortable environment for him to undertake his writing and research with easy access to Francis' notes and papers. His resolve to complete work based on Francis Willughby's research delayed, for some years, his own botanical publications.

Marriage

However, such are the unpredictable turn of events, Francis' death caused John to reflect on his future. He had up to this point lived a bachelor life. He had previously noted, in 1669, that all his friends were getting married and had remarked: "What is to become of me?"

The loneliness brought upon him by the loss of his friend gave him further opportunities to reflect on his future. This almost certainly led to his reflection on the relationship he had formed with Margaret Oakley, Governess to the Willughby children, daughter of John Oakley 'a Gentleman' who lived near Bicester in Oxfordshire.

John and Margaret, some 25 years younger, seem, at first sight and particularly in the disparity between their ages, an unlikely couple. Although little is known about their courtship, Raven recorded John's dilemma's recorded in the form of some brief notes John had written on the back of a letter. In summary the range of his thinking included the question of whether it was fair to burden a young woman of twenty with his bachelor ways, his religious beliefs and practice of prayer; as also his somewhat declining health. Then if they had children they "will never delight in my company for I shall be old before they have come to the years of discretion"

The situation in the household may have added tensions of its own as he pondered his future. There was also the embarrassment he would face if he asked Margaret if she would marry him and she refused. In the end he plucked up courage and asked her to be his wife to which she agreed. They were married on the 5th June 1673, eleven months after Francis' death.

This further turn in his fortunes was to give him a partner who would not only become the mother of their four children, all daughters, but provide him with the stability and support he required to undertake the most prolific period of writing in his life.

Their first years of marriage would have had difficulties in that they did not have a fixed home. There was also the fact that life in Middleton Hall was not easy, given Emma Willughby's apparent disdain of John. Is it possible that in some way she may have felt that the joint endeavours and travels of Francis and John were, in some way, connected to her husband's death? We shall probably never know. The news that he was to marry her children's governess is hardly likely to have improved relationships in the household, given the disparity in their ages and Emma's opinion of John. However events came to a head when Lady Cassandra, Francis' mother, died on the 25th July 1675 and the relationships in the household are said by Raven to have become very strained. Shortly after Emma married the wealthy Josiah Child.

At this point John had completed the work on the Ornithology he was to publish under Willughby's name. In the winter of 1675-6 John and Margaret went to Coleshill. In early 1676 the Ornithology was published and in April of that year they settled at Sutton Coldfield, four miles from Middleton. This allowed him still to have some access to Francis Willughby's collections and papers. The importance of having such access had probably been another one of the reasons he put up with the strained relationships in the household while he had remained in residence at Middleton Hall.

If it is thought that John's period at Middleton Hall and his work on the Ornithology might have led to his being somewhat forgotten on the public stage of academic significance then such a view is singularly wrong. In 1677 he was offered the Secretaryship of the Royal Society, evidence of his eminence as seen by his contemporaries. Although he was repeatedly urged to accept the position by his friends it is a testament to his character that he remained firm in not accepting it. He gave as his reason for refusal his need to complete a survey of botanical studies:

"There has not to my knowledge been published a general history of plants since Bauhinus'."

He was referring to the work Jean Bauhin (1541-1605) and his brother Gaspard (1560-1624) to which we will return later. It is also possible that his mind had already encompassed those future tasks, involving that monumental industriousness required to produce his published works about the natural world which would become the primary focus of his working life until his death in 1705.

Returning to the place of his birth

During their time at Sutton Coldfield John would also have been giving considerable thought to where he and Margaret were eventually going to settle and there was probably a growing urgency in his mind to resolve this dilemma. The decision was made to return to Essex and in November 1677 John and Margaret moved to Faulkbourne Hall, near Witham, about three miles from Black Notley and his mother's home. Faulkbourne Hall was lent to him by his friend Edward Bullock, while Edward was away. During his time there John produced an English version of Willughby's Ornithology, a second edition of his *Catalogus Angliae* and his book: *English Proverbs*.

On the 15th March 1679 his mother died: "In her house on Dewlands in the hall chamber about three of the clock in the afternoon, aged as I suppose seventy-eight."

John and Margaret subsequently moved, into his mother's house, in June of that year, the house he had had built some twenty-three years before. This was to be his final move, at the age of fifty-one. For the next twenty-four years it would be both his home and workplace and where his four daughters would be born.

As Raven described it, Dewlands was 'a larger edition' than the house John was born in, less than half a mile away. Constructed of lath and plaster, set in an oak frame it had a hall in the centre of the house with kitchen to the right and parlour to the left. A great fireplace was situated between these two rooms. In the kitchen was a staircase to the bedroom above and a passage giving access to another room above the hall.

On the left of the Hall approached though a door, was a passage running into a room at the back described as the brewhouse and scullery fitted with a copper. A door in the far side led back into the parlour and beyond it another staircase leading to the chambers over the parlour and brewhouse. The parlour had its own fireplace and chimney, as did the large room over the brewhouse, said to have been John's study and library.

Raven includes a footnote to the effect that J Vaughan, in an essay '*Essex and early Botanists*' says that this room was selected as it was the warmest room in the house. He is recorded as visiting the property in 1899 and being confirmed of this opinion. A fire destroyed Dewlands in 1900 and so we no longer have the opportunity to appraise it as we still have his birthplace.

Family man and natural scientist

What do we know of his work, family relationships and local friends over the remaining third of his life? We are aware of his prodigious output of work for publication and can marvel at the discipline and dedication required for such a task. We can also reflect on the nature of his marriage, commenced in somewhat difficult circumstances and now consolidated in their first and only home. The nature of his unremitting work in the preparation for publication of his detailed notes and studies suggests he would have required a wife who was highly supportive of his efforts and able to manage a household shortly to be doubled by the arrival of twin daughters.

In 1682, while he was still working on Willughby's History of fishes, John's *Methodus Plantarum*, a work dedicated to the classification of plants was published. He had made rapid progress on this important work since he had settled into Dewlands. However for many years previously he had given much thought and study to the importance of a system of plant classification. Raven describes how in the Preface to the book John admits to the limitation of any system of classification and the conditions under which he carried out his work:

"The number and variety of plants inevitably produce a sense of confusion in the mind of the student: but nothing is more helpful to clear understanding, prompt recognition and sound memory than a well ordered arrangement into classes, primary and subordinate. A method seemed to me useful to Botanists, especially beginners: I promised long ago to produce and publish one, and have now done so at the request of some friends. But I would not have my readers expect something perfect or complete: something which would divide all plants so exactly as to include every species without leaving any in positions anomalous or peculiar: something which would so define each genus by its own characteristics that no species be left, so to speak, homeless or be found common to many genera. Nature does not permit anything of the sort. Nature, as the saying goes, makes no jumps and passes from extreme to extreme only through a mean. She always produces species intermediate between higher and lower types, species of doubtful classification linking one type with another and having something in common with both-as for example the so-called Zoophytes between plants and animals.

In any case I dare not promise even so perfect a Method as nature permits-that is not the task of one man or of one age-but only such as I can accomplish in my present circumstances; and these are not too favourable. I have not myself seen or described all the species of plant now known. I live in the country far from London and Oxford and have no Botanical Gardens near enough to visit. I have neither time nor means for discovering, procuring and cultivating plants. Moreover botanical descriptions often omit or slur over the essential points that decide classification, flowers and seeds, calyces and seed vessels. So I have sometimes had to follow conjectures and set down rather what I surmised than what I knew."

This willingness to be honest about the limitations of his methodology is an example for all those engaged in science, recognising as it does the evolution of progress and achievement brought about by many contributors to the subject. Later we will demonstrate the underlying truth of this by looking at John's work set within the context of those who had proceeded him and the stages of learning and understanding they had reached before he came on the scene.

Two years after the publication of this work he became the father of twin daughters, Margaret and Mary, born on the 12th August 1684. One can imagine the wonder of all this for a man of nearly 57 and in the eleventh year of his marriage. This is not to mention the challenges of bringing up twin daughters against the requirements of unremitting study and concentration upon his work. That he was able to do so is probably a tribute to his wife Margaret and her management of the household in support of her perceived duties both to her husband and her children and their upbringing.

Less than two years later, in June 1686, the first volume of his greatest work *Historia Plantarum* was published. Ten months later his third daughter, Catherine, was born on the 3rd April 1687. The following year, 1688, the second volume of *Historia Plantarum* was published and on the 10th February 1689, Margaret gave birth to their fourth daughter, Jane.

One can imagine the family environment with four daughters under five years of age, demanding of the care and attention typical of infants and young children. How did the family cope and what sterling work was required by Margaret to keep the home in good order while John focussed on his studies and the prodigious output of work required for his publications. It is interesting to speculate on whether Margaret had help in the home and the extent to which John was able to break from his studies to help with the daily tasks of looking after such young children.

Whatever the stresses and strains of the household in March of 1690 John suffered a bout of pneumonia. In the same year he began a collection of insects. In 1691 he had published another of his famous works, the *Wisdom of God manifested in the Works of the Creation*. In 1692 a second edition of Wisdom was published and in 1693, when he was now 65 a further three publications related to a Synopsis of Quadrupeds, A Collection of Curious Travels and three Physico-Theological Discourses. Between the age of 67 and 68 he had another four works published.

By the end of 1697 he was 70 and his two eldest daughters 13 with Catherine 10 and Jane 8. Despite his declining health he had evidently much enjoyed their company as they accompanied him in the meadows in summertime helping him collect butterflies and insects for his studies. However a family tragedy was but a few months away.

Family tragedy

Early in January of 1698 Mary became ill with Chlorosis, an iron deficiency anaemia, rarely, on its own, in John's understanding of the condition fatal. However, Mary's condition became progressively worse and jaundiced. John was inclined to use his own herbal remedy for jaundice but deferred to their local Doctor, Dr Benjamin Allen, who lived in Braintree, less than three miles away. John had taken a liking to Doctor Allen, who had treated him for his pneumonia in 1690 as also Jane who at the same time had suffered what seems to have been an infant seizure. Allen had an interest in the natural world and discovered the male Glow-worm in 1692 followed by the deathwatch Beetle. This interest provided the two men with a sense of collaboration in Zoology. Such was their relationship that Margaret became Godmother to Allen's eldest son in 1697.

This relationship between the two men was to fracture over Allen's failure to treat Mary successfully combined with John' feeling of guilt that he had trusted the young Doctor when he felt confident that his own remedy might have proved successful. Mary' condition deteriorated and she died on the 29th January.

It is interesting to record the remedy that John would have used had he not placed his trust in Allen: "An infusion of stone horse dung steeped in ale for one night and with a little saffron added; the liquid then strained and sweetened with a little sugar and taken about half a pint at a time"

We can look back and feel that John's feelings of guilt and betrayal of trust, from our vantagepoint, were most certainly unfounded in the unlikely efficacy of his remedy. They remain a monument to his conscientiousness.

What sadness must have engulfed their household? In July of the same year they were again beset by the illnesses of his wife who was described as being very ill for some weeks and their daughter Margaret who presented similar symptoms of Jaundice and Chlorosis to that of Mary earlier in the year. Fortunately, she made a full recovery by the autumn.

By this time his own health was also causing him problems. From the age of 62 he had been suffering from blisters and chilblains, digestive problems and leg ulcers. These leg ulcers were clearly a major problem. He described them as "spreading and increasing and growing very deep and running extremely, being also so painful that they do very much hinder my rest; sometimes the heat and itching so violent that they force me to quit my bed."

In writing to one of his friends, Hans Sloane, in November 1699 he stated:
"I am in sad pain and have little heart to write or to do anything else; the days are so short that the forenoon is almost wholly spent in dressing my sores which are now more troublesome than ever."

Despite his afflictions his publications continued with his *Persuasive to a Holy Life* in 1700 and the third edition of *The Wisdom of God* in 1701. Two further publications followed in 1703 but in March of 1704 he became seriously ill. However in August his third and final volume of *Historia Plantarum* was published (The three volumes containing the descriptions of around 18,000 plants) as well as his *Methodus Insectorum* and the fourth edition of *Wisdom*.

However, as 1704 came to its close he was clearly in decline and he began to doubt that he would be well enough to complete '*The History of Insects*.' In November he wrote in a letter:

"The History of Insects must rest if I continue thus ill, and I see no likelihood of amendment unless I overlive this winter." On the 7th January 1705 he wrote his last letter to his friend Hans Sloane:

"These are to take a final leave of you as of this world. I look upon myself as a dying man. God requite your kindness expressed anyways towards me an hundredfold, bless you with a confluence of all good things in this world and eternal life and happiness hereafter, and grant us a happy meeting in heaven"

On Wednesday the 17th January 1705, at 10.00 in the morning, he died.

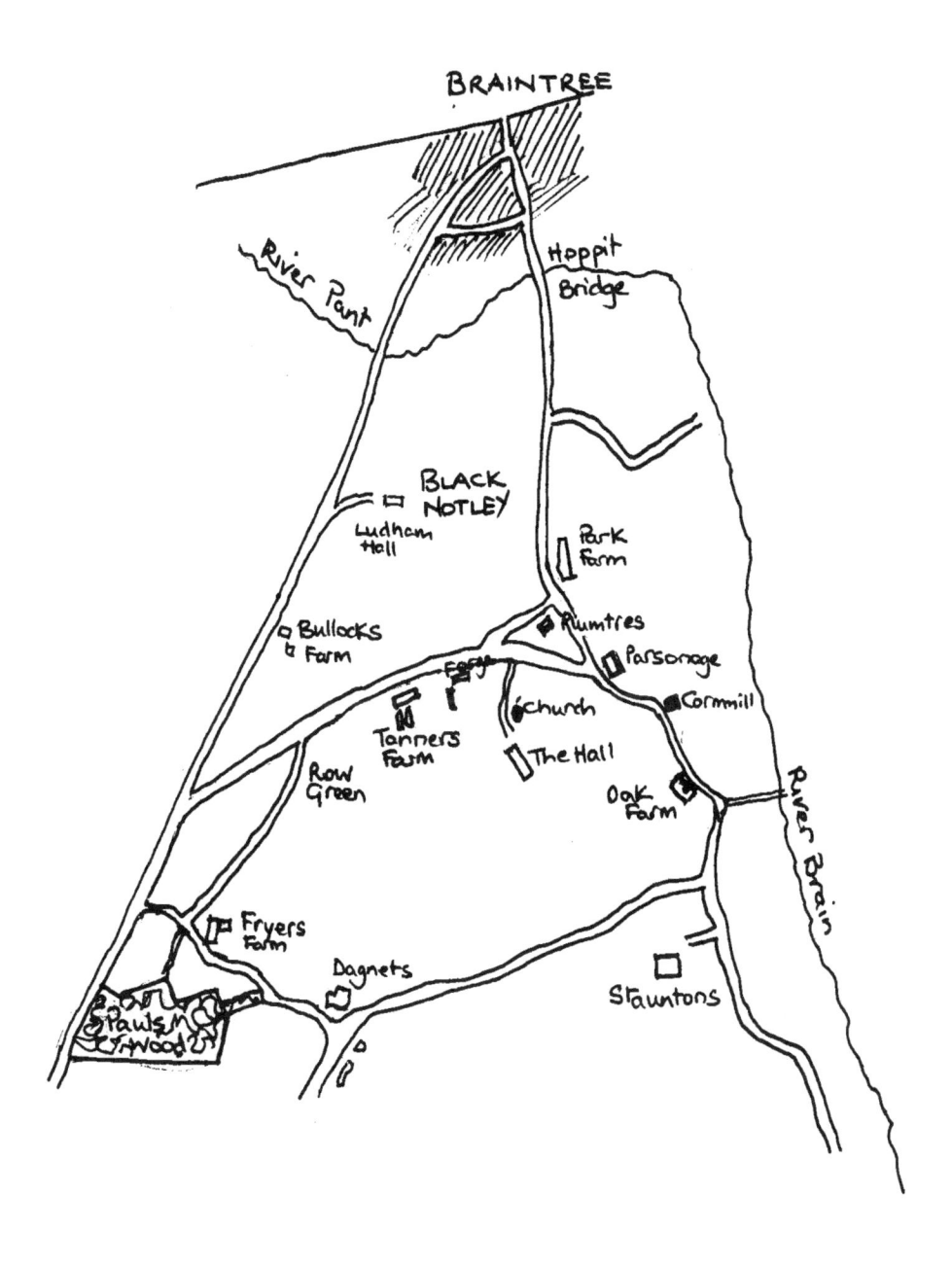

Above: Black Notley Parish, 18th century

Above and below: John Ray Cottage and Forge, Black Notley.
Drawn by Bob Vickers.

"HOUSE, SMITHY, GARDEN" – BLACK NOTLEY
FIELD N° 279 TITHE LISTING 1838
– Where John RAY was born

Bob VICKERS.

Above: Dewlands where John Ray lived and died. The house burnt down in 1900. Drawn by Bob Vickers

Below left: The Wedgewood Portrait. A Medallion of John Ray struck to commemorate his death in 1705. Attributed to G. Gaab.

Right: John Ray's tomb, in the churchyard at St Peter & St Paul's Church, Black Notley. Drawn by Bob Vickers

Part Two
Predecessors in the Natural Sciences

Although John Ray entered a western world where the emergence of scientific method was the stage upon which he was to play a leading role, it is a fallacy to believe that previously little of merit had been undertaken or written about in the natural sciences. Indeed one of the main purposes of this book is to demonstrate how his work was a natural, albeit significant, continuation of the work of his predecessors. As I hope to show he adopted and took forward many already identified principles related to working methods that sometimes have come to be attributed to his creation. That his unique genius contributed to the major development of the natural sciences is not in dispute and the chapter on his specific contribution will demonstrate this. But it is important, before we look at this, to examine the work of those who had gone before him.

Aristotle (384-322 BC) wrote an account of animals (*Historia Animalium*) in which he attempted to include all previous knowledge of past learning. He established groupings known today as Vertebrates and Invertebrates and distinguished birds, fishes, amphibians and reptiles.

Theophrastus (371-287 BC) would appear to be the first person to provide Botany with a scientific basis. In his account of plants (*Historia Plantarum*) and his origin of plants (*Causae Plantarum*) he looked at the distinctive characteristics of plants related to their environment, their methods of production and life cycles. As with Aristotle he attempted to summarise all previous work known to him on the subject.

He dealt with plant description and classification dividing plants into four groups: trees, shrubs, undershrubs and herbs.

Little further work appears to have been undertaken by western Scholars for the following fifteen hundred years until the Renaissance. (14-16th centuries) save for the recorded work of Dioscorides believed to have been a Greek physician working with the Roman Army around 60 AD. He produced a *Materia Medica* identifying around 1000 drugs of use to human beings over half of which were derived from plants.

The diminution in the work and renown of western scholars during this fifteen hundred-year period was almost certainly related to the decline of the Greek and Roman civilisations and the Roman withdrawal from conquered territories. In Britain the Roman withdrawal was followed by the settling of Angles and Saxons, then by Vikings and Normans. All these peoples with different languages and cultures must have had its impact on the development of scholarship.

The emergence of Islam, in Arabia, in the seventh century and the spread of Islamic culture resulted in centres of learning being established as far apart as Baghdad in the East to Toledo in the West from which the Islamic contribution to the history of science could be continued and advanced. Muslim scholars translated versions of Greek texts into Arabic and added their own significant contributions and developments in mathematics, chemistry, optics and astronomy. One of their important roles, from the perspective of the western world, was to preserve and make more widely known the work of Greek philosophy and science so that it could be used by European scholars from the tenth century onwards. Over the next two hundred years Latin translations were made from Arabic, facilitating the gathering together of scholars across Europe where new Latin versions of ancient texts could be discussed in centres that were to become universities.

Left: St Michael's Church. In the 17th century the Grammar School was held in the Jesus Chapel

Above: Hoppit Mead, Braintree. Ray walked across this area on his way to school. He recalled seeing the Wild Blackcurrant growing here.

John Ray walked this way to school, held in St Michael's Church

Above: The Chapel, Trinity College.
Photographed by Janet Turner

Above: Ray's home at Middleton Hall, a small annexe building

Right: Faulkbourne Hall, home of Edward Bullock. This house was lent to John and Margaret Ray in 1677.

There then followed significant developments in mathematics through Leonardo Fibonacci, in the late eleventh and twelfth century, making for the acceptance of decimals using Arabic numerals. Then there was the work of the German astronomers George van Purbach and Johannes Muller in the fifteenth century, when they developed trigonometrical and astronomical tables. These led to new scientific understanding and capability.

Perhaps the most significant development was the invention of the printing press, in the late fifteenth century, by Johannes Gutenberg, dramatically facilitating access to learning. All these developments together meant that those in pursuit of scientific understanding and development could share their work as never before.

In the sixteenth Century the Swiss botanist, Gesner, (1516-1565) studied some 250 authors to compile all that was known about animals attempting to separate fact from myth. At the time of his death he was working on a general history of plants that included 1500 drawings, illustrating details of the flower, fruit and seed of each plant.

One of the great contributors to botany in the sixteenth century was the Italian Cesalpino (1519-1603) who made the first significant advances in the science of plant classification, acknowledging the work of Theophrastus who had written on the subject some seventeen hundred years previously. His contribution was in the anatomy and physiology of plants, emphasising the function of the root and stem.

In Ray's own assessment one of the primary influences upon him was the work of Jean Bauhin (1541-1605) a Frenchman who studied Botany in Germany with Gesner. His major work *Historia Plantarum Universalia* (An account of the plants of the world) was completed and published after his death. John described it thus:

"It contained almost everything that is worthy of record in both ancient and modern writings together with synonyms and critical comment."

Jean's younger brother, Gaspard Bauhin (1560-1624) recognised the developing problem of different names being given to the same species by different authors. In his *Pinax Theatri Botanici*, published in 1623, he named some 6,000 species providing the names used in previous publications that were synonymous. In his nomenclature (system of names) he used descriptive binomial names comprising a generic and then specific name. (e.g. he named the potato: Solanum Tuberosum). John Ray later adopted his nomenclature.

John would certainly also have been influenced by the work of Jung (1587-1657) a professor of Natural Science at Hamburg. John is known to have seen a manuscript of his guide to examining plants in 1660, later published in 1669 (*Isagogue Phystoscopica*). Jung developed Cesalpino's work of plant classification. He divided the plant into a number of integral and vital parts devising a new descriptive terminology later used by John Ray.

Of particular interest to John would have been any work that advanced the knowledge of plants with medicinal applications, known as Herbals. His early years, accompanying his mother searching for such plants in the meadows surrounding their home were the foundation stones of his love of nature and he would have followed the history of their development at every opportunity that presented itself.

Reference has been made to Discorides, the Greek Physician with the Roman Army, who in 60AD identified over 500 drugs derived from plants. But what was the original medical theory behind the use of Herbals? Put simply it was believed by classical scholars that the health of human beings was dependant upon the correct balance of four Humours: Blood, Phlegm, Choler and Meloncholy – each humour corresponding to one of the elements: Fire, Air, Water and earth. Each had two characteristics: whether dry or moist and whether cold or hot.

According to the theory, human sickness was caused when these humours were out of balance. Plants provided the means of remedying this situation as they also contained humours. Treatment consisted of the physician needing to diagnose which plant contained the opposite humour to correct the balance and in determining the amount or dose needed so as not to over or under dose the sufferer.

Although on first reading this may seem a far-fetched theory, on further reflection, it encompasses the process of modern diagnosis and prescription, albeit now, with the understanding that there are many different causative factors that have been identified in the course of medical research and discovery. Today drugs with plant derivatives remain in regular and widespread use as part of the chemotherapy treatment options used by doctors.

One of the most eminent Herbalists of the sixteenth century was William Turner (1508-1568) whose life may be said to have similarities with that of John Ray. He too was educated at Cambridge, where he studied medicine, turning to the study of botany in his leisure time. Turner also travelled on the continent where he met other naturalists including Gesner. He later published *A New Herbal* in three parts (1551, 1562 and 1568). His work starts by describing all the plants known to the Greeks and Romans and then all those identified since then.

As Stuart Baldwin describes in his book: *John Ray – Essex Naturalist* (1986) Turner identified some 238 native herbal plants and his book became the standard botanical medical text for many years. Of particular interest is his parallel experience to that of John with regard to the lack of awareness of botany in Cambridge:

" I could never learn one Greek, neither Latin nor English name, even among physicians, of any herb or tree.."

Turner made it his duty to enable English physicians to know their herbs. It is interesting to record, with an eye to John Ray's own work, that Turner went to some lengths to provide accurate descriptions, details of locality and names in English, Latin, Greek, German and French which had not been done previously.

Other notable Herbalists leading up to John Ray's time included Johnson (Circa 1605-1644) who was a London Apothecary and published an account of the plants found in Hampstead Heath and Kent that seems to have been the first account of British Flora. He planned a much more extensive work, covering all British plants but this was prevented by his early death.

Parkinson (1567-1650) was Botanist to Charles I and a famous gardener, reputed to be the first person to publish an English Gardening book. He also published: *Theatrum Botanicam* (The Theatre of Plants) attempting to describe all known plants which were classified on the basis of their uses and qualities. It included references and learning from the Bauhin brothers and it is believed that John Ray studied it in detail.

We can see, therefore, that as John Ray emerged onto the scene of the seventeenth century, the inheritance from his predecessors greatly facilitated his work. He embraced many of their working methods and principles of work that he was to make his own and for which he is rightly held in such high regard.

Part Three
An Appreciation of John Ray's Contribution in the Natural Sciences

One of he first publication of the Ray Society, in 1846, was a book entitled *Memorials of John Ray*. In the preface to the book the editor, Edwin Lankester, wrote these words:
'The extent of the influence of the genius of Ray on the science of natural history is far greater than can be estimated by the number or size of the volumes which he wrote, and is to be traced to his habit of acute observation of facts and the logical accuracy with which he arranged them. He made his knowledge of the structure and physiology of plants subservient to a great plan for their arrangement, and this plan, when carefully examined, will be found to contain the fundamental principles of all the more recent scientific systems in natural history, and to have laid the foundation of the views of a natural classification of the vegetable kingdom put forward in later times'

    Writing one hundred and fifty six years later, in 2002, in his book *Science A History*, John Gribbin wrote:
'It was Ray who, more than anybody else, made the study of botany and zoology a scientific pursuit, bringing order and logic to the investigation of the living world out of the chaos that existed before. He invented a clear taxonomic system based on physiology, morphology and anatomy, thereby paving the way for the work of the much more famous Linnaeus, who drew heavily (without always acknowledging the debt) on the work published by Ray.'

    What was it about John Ray that set him apart from his contemporaries and resulted in such high commendation spanning the 300 years since his death? We have already included Raven's observation, made in 1942, concerning John's extraordinary ability to gain knowledge from his observations of plants for the *Cambridge Catalogue* (1660). Such ability was enhanced by his energy, methodical and orderly approach, aptitude for and love of the natural world.

It is clear that he felt he had a duty to God to undertake this work in recognition of the beauty and awesome complexity of creation in which he saw the hand of a Divine designer:

"To illustrate the Glory of God in the knowledge of the works of nature or Creation"

Botany

In a practical way and with a pragmatic approach he transformed the situation he found in the publications and manuscripts of his predecessors where duplications, jumbled synonyms and obscure descriptions abounded. He realised that he had to bring order to this situation before he could proceed with a system of plant classification.

His honesty and humility, notwithstanding his evident ability, were vital and integral factors in his genius as a scientist, qualities that are as essential now as they were then. His approach was that of a person aware of his limitations and the limitations of what could be discovered and understood in his times. He therefore always proceeded with caution, acknowledging the inherent imperfections that are inextricably part of human exploration, hypothesis and achievement.

His view of scientific development is that it was something to explore, find out about and make sense of. His eleven years of travel throughout this country and especially on the continent where he was able to study the works of predecessors and contemporaries was clearly not only a broadening experience but one that stimulated his imagination and developed his scientific perspective.

The focus of his work, the systemisation of nature, was clearly fired by his student and great friend Francis Willughby whose early death probably reinforced his commitment to the completion of this lifetime's work. Their commitment to visit the locations wherein species were located combined with John's detailed notes made as a result of accurate observation built up an archive upon which he could draw in later years and match against what he read and studied from the works of others.

Another aspect of his commitment to a scientific approach is in the extension of his work and his determination to improve, update and enhance understanding. In 1670 his *Catalogus Plantarum Angliae* (Catalogue of English Plants) contained sections not included in the Cambridge Catalogue published ten years earlier. He included a section devoted to the importance and definition of species, stressing the need for this and linking their unique medical properties. He provided a large index at the back of the book containing a list of diseases, symptoms and pharmacological actions with the appropriate plants to use for each. (e.g. for epilepsy he lists six plants, seven for angina, and some 47 as diuretics)

This systematic approach to his work effectively demonstrated the superiority of scientific method over superstition, very much still the order of the day in his times.

His enthusiasm was another enriching quality he brought to his work. On his continental tour, everywhere he went, he made lists of the plants he found:

"Whether my readers will enjoy these bare lists of names, I do not know: to me to gaze at the plants themselves freely growing on the lavish bosom of mother earth was an unbelievable delight: I can say with Clusius that I was as pleased to find for the first time a new plant as if I had received a fortune"

One of Raven's other valid points is that, because of his extensive travels, John Ray had probably seen a larger number of wild plants than any other contemporary botanist thereby making him a master of his subject.

John Ray's greatest contribution to Botany is generally accepted as his improvement to plant classification. In order to improve his knowledge and understanding of plants he conducted experiments to learn about their physiology and growth embracing therefore both the descriptive and experimental aspects of scientific method.

In his paper to the Royal Society on the 17th December 1674 'On the seeds of Plants' he demonstrated that some plants have two seed leafs and others only one. (Dicotyledons and Monocotyledons). In a second paper delivered on the same day 'The specific Difference of Plants' he established precise criteria for determining a species. He indicated that such criteria did not include size, colour, smell, taste, shape or variegation. His criteria stressed the overall structural morphology of the plant.

He identified the principal parts of the plant as the Flower, Calyx, Seed and Seed Vessel, because they are consistent and do not vary. He was the first person to use the term Petal for the coloured leaf of a flower.

His work-rate was prolific. As Raven commented on the effort required to produce the first volume of his *Historia Plantarum*. It contained:

'984 numbered pages, an endless series of descriptions, a multitude of references and took three years of writing.....In the early chapters of volume 1 he produced a detailed up to date textbook of botanical science covering all that was known on Anatomy, Physiology, Reproduction, Morphology and Classification....he laid the foundations for future studies in plant physiology outlining details of the movement of water as a major feature of transpiration in plants.....In his *Historia* Ray shows his genius for abstracting and summarising the best of all that had gone before him, coupling with it his own massive and unique contribution and synthesising it into a coherent whole, resulting in a clear, succinct and masterly exposition of current botanical knowledge...thereby laying one of the great foundation stones on which modern botanical science is based."

All this would have been enough to provide him with a lasting legacy but his achievements in Zoology were equally outstanding.

Zoology

Given the time required for his botanical studies and writings it is remarkable how he found the time to undertake significant and pioneering work in Zoology, writing books on Birds, Fishes, Mammals, Reptiles and Insects. His commitment to finishing Willughby's work on birds probably set him on a course that he was anxious to pursue and apply that developing scientific methodology so characteristic of his work.

Along with all pioneering scientists he studied all the previous literature, discarding that which he felt to be irrelevant or based on superstition. As with his major work on plants he collated names and descriptions and established natural criteria for species based upon significant structural features, adding his own acute power of observation and genius for description. This was later described by Gilbert White as unrivalled.

Newton, in *A Dictionary of Birds* (1893-96) wrote:
" The foundations of Scientific Ornithology were laid by the joint labours of Francis Willughby and John Ray"
John described how they set about the task in the Objects of the *Ornithologiae*:
"Our main design was to illustrate the history of birds, which is (as we said before of animals in general) in many particulars confused and obscure, by so accurately describing each kind, and observing their characteristics and distinctive notes, that the reader might be sure of meaning, and upon comparing any bird with our description not fail of discerning whether it be described or no.....We did not as some before us have done, only transcribe other men's descriptions, but we ourselves did carefully describe each bird from the view and inspection before us".

In so doing they corrected the mistakes of previous writers, particularly in respect of the many names and descriptions then in current use.

"Their mistakes are especially in the multiplying of species and making two or three sorts of one." Raven, who was an experienced Ornithologist, commented (1942): "He had based his system upon accurate study and dissection; he had tried to take the whole life and structure of each species into account, he has given us the first scientific classification"

As Baldwin commented in his book in 1986, the classification used by John Ray was a considerable advance on anything that had gone before and bore the stamp of his knowledge of anatomy and the importance of the relationship between form and function. Baldwin also reveals how John had an extensive anatomical knowledge of birds having carried out dissections from his early days in Cambridge and especially during his continental tour.

The work of the *Ornithologiae*, largely attributed to John Ray but which he published under Willughby's name, inspired a whole succession of later scholars including Linnaeus, Buffon and Gilbert White. As Raven stated (1942):

"The book itself will always remain an object of reverence to the ornithologist and of admiration to the historian. When we consider the confusion of its predecessors, the short time and scanty material available to its authors, and the difficulties of the subject, in days when collecting and observation had none of their modern instruments, the quality of the achievement stands out."

Studies of Fishes

John Ray's work on fishes was again linked to his association with Francis Willughby. He had helped Francis prepare a table of fishes for Wilkins' publication entitled Real Character. Wilkins was a Bishop and a member of the Royal Society. John also produced two appendices for Wilkins' *Collection of English Words* published in 1673, which were catalogues of *Fish from near Penzance and St Ives*, and *Freshwater Fish Found in England*. Baldwin explains that the material came from the observations John had made on his travels; another illustration of the meticulous nature of his work and its breadth.

After completing the Ornithologiae, John started work on the History of Fishes. Again he followed his usual method of reading and examining the work of previous authorities involving a great many more publications than those published about birds.

Baldwin notes that his main sources were Rondelet's *De Piscibus Marinis*, published in France in 1554 and Salviani's *Aquatilium Animalium Historiae* published in Italy in the same year. Many of the best plates used by John in his publication *Historia Piscium,* eventually published in 1686, originated from the work of Salviani.

It was while he was working on the History of Fishes that John had to leave Middleton Hall, following the remarriage of Emma Willughby. His access to Willughby's notes then became problematic but with his typical perseverance and with the help of friends he completed the work.

Emma Willughby's second marriage led to a further problem in that John was left without the necessary funding for the publication, especially the cost of the plates. But for the intervention of a friend, Dr Tancred Robinson, the manuscript would possibly have been left unpublished. However Robinson drew the attention of the Royal Society to it in 1685 and the Society agreed to publish it. Samuel Pepys, as president, contributed £50 to pay for 79 plates and many others, including Christopher Wren, Robert Boyle, John Evelyn and Elias Ashmole followed his example.

Within twelve months the *History of Fishes* was published, the same year as his first volume of *Historia Plantarum* (1686). As Baldwin states (1986) *Historia Piscium* was a folio production in which many of the 187 plates were of high quality. The most accurate being engraved from recent drawings of fresh specimens. The

Historia was comprised of four books the first included the definition of a fish and several chapters on anatomical details including the function of the air bladder, reproduction, food, age, growth and classification.

Raven (1942) quotes John's own reflections of the work:

"We have...attempted...only to record the observations of ourselves or our friends or of reliable authorities. We shrink from unnecessary multiplication of species, and to avoid it have visited all the chief fishing ports of England, and the markets of Belgium, Germany, Italy and France; have bought all the species new to us and described them so that the reader can easily recognise them. We cannot claim to have found many new species; we have found some and can claim to have described, discriminated and classified more accurately"

This concise yet comprehensive summation of his work on the history of fishes amply reveals the meticulousness of his methodology as well as the extent of his travels, undertaken to ensure his observations and descriptions were as accurate as possible.

Synopsis of Animals and Reptiles

Baldwin's excellent book on John Ray's work goes on to describe John's work on animals and reptiles seemingly in response to Tancred Robinson's exhortation in a letter sent to John in 1684:

"I am in great hopes that you will bestow on the world a general history of nature; it is very defective at present, and seems to call for method and perfection from you"

John published a synopsis of animals and reptiles in 1693 – *Synopsis Methodica Animalium Quadrupedum Et Serpentini Generis*. As Baldwin points out, although John had undertaken a considerable amount of dissection work at Cambridge and Italy and had knowledge of physiology from his reading, this was a comparatively new area of study for him.

At this point in his life, however, he had consolidated his understanding and practice of scientific method and he knew how best to set about the work. This not only included knowing what to look for in the work of predecessors or contemporaries but also in applying the principles of classification. As a measure of his achievement Baldwin quotes the observations on the work by Thomas Pennant almost ninety years later:
"...So correct was his genius that we see a systematic arrangement arising even from the chaos of Aldrovandi and Gesner. Under his hand the indigested matter of those able and copious writers assumes a new form, and the whole is made clear and perspicuous."

Typical of his methodological approach John started his work with an explanation of what an animal is and although there were defects in the system of classification he used, based on Aristotle's method, his work was considered to be a significant scientific advance laying a foundation for future systematic zoology. Baldwin quotes Gregory writing in 1910:
"Ray may justly be regarded as the founder of modern zoology. He was the great figure of the seventeenth century, as was Linnaeus of the eighteenth"

Insects

As a young boy accompanying his mother in the search for plants with medicinal properties and from the dawning of his love of nature John would have become aware of the many forms of insects. In his Cambridge catalogue when describing Sopewart he added this note:
" One of the papilio media (Butterflies) of Mouffet.....Delights to sit on this plant in the month of August; it is notable not only for its very swift flight but also for its very long proboscis and the loud noise which it emits, almost like that of a hornet."

During the period of his travels and collecting he had predominantly left the subject of insects to Willughby. His other commitments prevented him from starting work on insects until 1690 when he was in his early sixties. He was also unable to gain access to Francis Willughby's notes in 1704, the year before he died. Unlike the other areas of his studies, previously published works on insects appear to have been limited and the two main sources of his study were Moffet's *Insectorum Theatrum* (Theatre of Insects) produced in 1634 and Swammerdam's *History of Insects*, (1669).

Another contrast was that he was now infirm and dependent on others to provide him with material for his work. As Baldwin explains, he relied for some of his specimens on friends and correspondents including Samuel Dale, a local doctor. However, the majority of his specimens were obtained by his wife and daughters and a Thomas Simpson, who Raven suggests may have been a servant in the Ray household, who collected caterpillars, moths, butterflies and other insects within a three-mile radius of their home.

His usual energy applied to the sorting, describing and classifying the large number of insects identified was no longer available to him and his main work *Historia Insectorum* was unfinished at his death. His preliminary Classification was published in 1705, the year of his death, as a small ten-page catalogue entitled *Methodus Insectorum*. None the less the notes he left behind provided enough information for an editor to ensure the full work could be published in 1710.

Having discussed the limitations besetting him in this final work, *Historia Insectorum* contained the details of numerous new species. It also contained the basis of a classification and a considerable volume of information on many insect groups including butterflies, moths, beetles, wasps, flies, bugs, fleas, ticks, worms, leeches, spiders, millipedes, dragonflies, bees and grasshoppers. All this from a man in failing health.

As a further example of his industriousness in the face of his increasing frailty was his describing the complete life cycle of 47 species of butterfly from egg to imago. His famous and inspirational prose sums up his view of them: "You ask what is the use of butterflies? I reply to adorn the world and delight the eyes of men: to brighten the countryside like so many golden jewels. To contemplate their exquisite beauty and variety is to experience the truest pleasure. To gaze enquiringly at such elegance of colour and form designed by the ingenuity of nature and painted by her artist's pencil, is to acknowledge and adore the imprint of the art of God."

The final sentence of this quotation of beautifully descriptive prose leads us to reflect on the underlying purpose John Ray ascribed to the relationship between his religious beliefs and his life's work as discussed in Part Four of this book.

Geology and Fossils

Before discussing the integral relationship between John Ray's beliefs in theology and science it is instructive to look at his work in geology and palaeontology. There can be little doubt that it demonstrates both the extent of his advanced scientific thinking as well as his ability to challenge previously held scientific and contemporary religious views over the age and development of the Earth.

Nicholas Steno, born in 1638 and therefore eleven years younger than John Ray, is acknowledged as the first person to claim that evidence of the earth's past was to be found in rocks. Despite the fact that he went on to become a bishop of the Roman Catholic Church, he effectively displaced the bible as the only accepted authority on the subject. His work can rightly be argued as having transformed Western civilisation's previous understanding of the history and nature of the Earth from a static to dynamically evolving phenomenon.

Previously, dependence on a literal biblical interpretation of the age of the Earth was defended vigorously and most educated people of Steno's day believed that fossil shells grew where they were found or were the remains of the great deluge of Noah's time. The Ancient Greeks had believed otherwise as Steno was to demonstrate.

John Ray had met Steno on his continental tour and was aware of his ideas, which accorded with his own developing viewpoint. His earliest published work on the subject was his *Observations,* 1673, to be followed much later in 1692 by *Miscellaneous Discourses.* In his earlier publication he made the following observation concerning the origin of fossils, indicative of his advanced thinking:

"The first and most probable opinion is that they were originally the Shells or Bones of living Fishes and other Animals bred in the Sea"

He then cites Steno as indicating that this was the "general opinion of the Ancients", referring to the Greek scholars.

John Ray then goes on to challenge conventional thinking by stating:

"….either the world is a great deal older than is imagined or believed.. or that in the primitive times and soon after the Creation the earth suffered far more concussions and mutations in its superficial part than afterwards"

Later in the same work he spells out what he believes had happened: "First of all it will hence follow that all the earth was once covered by the Sea" and "If it be said that these Shells were brought in by the universal deluge in the time of Noah, when the mountains were covered, I answer, that the deluge proceeded from Rain, which was more likely to carry shells down to the Sea, than bring them up from it"

Also in *Observations* he states: "That many years ago before all records of antiquity these places were part of the firm land and covered with wood; afterwards being overwhelmed by the violence of the sea they continued so long under water till the rivers brought down earth and mud enough to cover the trees, fill up these shallows and restore them to firm land again."

Baldwin argues that Ray's essay in *Observations* was a highly significant contribution to the development of geological science well in advance of most of his contemporaries. Additionally that his studies in geology and into the origins of fossils place him, alongside Steno, as one of the founders of geological science. The extent of his work on fossils and geology is set out in chapter XVI of Raven's detailed biography.

Part Four
Theology and Science

John Ray's work in the natural sciences was, in his eyes, the living out of his destiny. He saw it as his duty to put to work those unique talents that had been bestowed upon him. His belief in God is best explained in his own eloquent words:

"For you may hear....persons affirming, that they need no proof of the being of a God, for that every pile of grass, or ear of corn, sufficiently proves that...for...all the men in the world cannot make such a thing as one of these; and if they cannot do it, who can, or did make it but God? To tell them that it made itself, or sprung up by chance, would be as ridiculous as to tell the greatest philosopher so"

Again:

"A wonder then.... That there should be any man found so stupid and forsaken of reason, as to persuade himself, that this most beautiful and adorned world was or could ever be produced by the fortuitous concurrence of atoms."

The above quotations are taken from his famous work: *The Wisdom of God Manifested in the Works of Creation* published in 1691. He continues his affirmation in authoritative tone:

"Secondly, the particulars of this Discourse serve not only to demonstrate the Being of a Deity, but to illustrate some of his principal attributes; namely, his infinite Power and Wisdom. The vast multitude of creatures and those not only small, but immensely great, the Sun and the Moon, and all the heavenly host, are effects and proofs of his almighty Power.....The admirable contrivance of all and each of them, the Adapting all the Parts of Animals to their several uses, The Provision that is made for their sustenance...They serve to stir up and increase in us the Affection and Habits of Admiration, Humility, and Gratitude"

Here we see in these quotations how his belief in God is inextricably linked with his perception of the natural world.

In 1999 Professor R Berry prepared a paper entitled *'John Ray, Father of Natural Historians'* for the conference 'John Ray and his Successors.'

He identified the three core beliefs that John applied to his life and work:

" 1. The Earth belongs to God
2. He has entrusted it to us to care for on his behalf
3. He will hold us responsible for our discharge of this trust"

Berry went on to show how this belief was central to beliefs in our recent times by quoting from a Church of England General Synod Paper (Christians and the Environment, 1991):

"We all share and depend on the same world…Christians believe that this world belongs to God by creation, redemption and sustenance, and that he has entrusted it to humankind…. responsible to him; we are in the position of stewards, tenants, curators, trustees or guardians, whether or not we acknowledge this responsibility. Stewardship implies caring management…. It involves a concern for both the present and future…"

John Ray would have endorsed this view. Towards the end of *'The Wisdom of God…'* he discusses the human condition:

"First let us give thanks to Almighty God for the Perfection and Integrity of our Bodies. It would not be amiss to put it into the Eucharistical part of our daily Devotions: We praise thee oh God, for the due number, Shape, and use of our Limbs and Senses; and in general, of all the parts of our Bodies; we bless thee for the sound and healthful Constitution of them"

In talking of the human tongue he reveals the extent of his faith and how, for him, the understanding of it was embedded in his thoughts feelings and actions:

"You will say to me, How then must our Tongues be employed; I answer,
1. In Praises and Thanksgiving unto God

2. We must exercise our Tongues in talking of his wondrous works
3. In Prayer to God
4. In Confession of Him, and his Religion, and publicly owning it before Men, whatever the Hazard be.
5. In Teaching, Instructing, and Counselling of others
6. In Exhorting them
7. In Comforting them that need it
8. In Reproving them"

He then goes on to talk about his belief in the Soul:

"Let us hence learn duly to prize and value our Souls....The Body is but a husk or shell, the Soul is the Kernel; The Body but the Cask, the Soul the precious Liquor contained in it; the body is But the Cabinet, the Soul the Jewel; the Body is but the Ship or Vessel, The Soul the Pilot; the Body is but the Tabernacle, and a poor clay Tabernacle or Cottage too, The Soul the Inhabitant...."

And:

"You will say, how shall we manifest our Care of our Souls? What shall we do for them? I answer the same we do for our bodies. First we feed our Bodies, our Souls are also to be fed: The food of the Soul is Knowledge, especially knowledge in the Things of God, and the Things that concern its Eternal Peace and Happiness; the Doctrine of Christianity, the Word of God read and preached........Knowledge is the Foundation of Practice; it is impossible to do God's will before we know it; the Word must be received into an honest and good heart and understood, before any Fruit can be brought forth"

These few quotations illustrate his beliefs and how he sees the practice of them. There is much more detail in *'The Wisdom of God...'* relating to his beliefs and how they should be applied, including numerous Biblical references, illustrating the depth of his theological understanding.

This is a seventeenth century man, full of faith in God and yet breaking new boundaries in Scientific Method, one of the towering minds of his times. He is alert to the dangers of intellectual arrogance, yet firmly embedded to what he sees as the eternal truths. His work in the natural sciences, he views, as an adventure of exploration, observation, description and classification. He is fully aware of the limitations of human capability and achievement within his lifetime and is able to look forward to a future, long after his demise, when existing knowledge and understanding will be expanded.

In his book 'The Puzzle of God' (1999) Peter Vardy, a lecturer in the Philosophy of Religion, states: " Science and Theology both end in unexplained mysteries and both, at their best, should be willing to pursue an open-minded search into the unknown"

This statement follows his review of philosophical beliefs challenged by scientific discoveries and opinions from Aristotle, Aquinas and up to and including the current works of Richard Dawkins. John Polkinghorne, a mathematical physicist, in his book, *One World the interaction of science and theology* (1986), also argues in similar terms stating that what science and theology have in common is that they are both concerned with and involved in the search for truth related to our understanding of reality.

Polkinghorne reiterated, in *Science and Creation the search for understanding* (1988), that natural theology is the search for God through the use of reason and study of the world or put even more simply, the search for understanding. Polkinghorne also states that the search for unity of knowledge that physicists seek, in order to establish a 'Grand Unified Theory,' will eventually lead beyond physics to theology.

St Anselm's definition of theology is: "Fides quaerens intellectum" - Faith seeking understanding. And again: "I do not understand in order to believe but believe in order to understand."

John Ray would almost certainly have agreed with all these views. His was not a static view of creation but one that could see, if not fully understand, that adaptation and development of species was in some way related to environmental circumstances. I believe he would have whole

heartedly agreed with the definition of Science made by Thomas Crump in his book 'A brief History of Science as seen through the development of Scientifc Instruments' (2001):
"Science is the aggregate of systematised and methodical knowledge concerning nature, developed by speculation, observation and experiment, so leading to objective laws governing phenomena and their explanation. The process is one of trial and error, so that the 'objective laws' are not necessarily correct. The historical process consists very largely of established laws being replaced by new ones...."

And later:

" ...the history of science is itself largely a chapter of errors. But then as G.K Chesterton once said, 'a man who has never made a mistake has never made anything.' "

Casting our minds back to speculate and imagine the state of the emerging species, Homo Sapiens, it is clear that the development of language was a fundamental part of sharing understanding about specific dangers and needs and identifying them by means of a familiar and repeated sound. The classification of things would have inevitably followed this process and the need to improve such understanding has been a feature of our development as a species. Trial and error, speculation and testing out or experimenting are therefore inherent in our survival behaviour.

This basic appreciation of a fundamental aspect of human evolution has been understood almost from the beginning although it was probably more instinctive in our early ancestors compared to the much greater cognitive awareness of present times.

For John Ray it was how he approached his work, believing that the tools of accurate observation and careful description combined with an orderly and methodical approach was his way of learning more about the functioning of God's creatures and the natural environment.

As Raven (1942) states of John Ray:
"He had learnt from his own studies the lesson which his teachers had outlined, that reason, strictly disciplined and honestly followed, was the supreme instrument in science and religion... that loyalty to truth was loyalty to God; and that man derived his status from his capacity to share in and respond to Divine wisdom.....He had received a mental and religious training which invested his scientific researches with the dignity of a sacred calling.....he had accepted as his vocation the task of 'thinking God's thoughts after Him'.....there was for him nothing incongruous in seeing the objects of his study, the order of the universe, the life of plants and animals, the structure and functioning of nature, as the manifestation of the mind of God. Indeed the wonder with which he regarded the works of creation, and the thrill which accompanied his growing insight into the process of their growth and function, were to him, as to mankind in general, essentially religious."

As a seventeenth century man John Ray was surrounded by weaknesses in many traditional beliefs that have become exposed, by advances in science, and have required a different or alternative explanation. It is Raven's view that John Ray was aware of this and as Raven comments:
"He worked within a framework of contemporary Christian thought, but with a loyalty to experiment and observation and a faith in the unity and rationality of nature which contributed powerfully to the abandonment of that framework and stimulated the quest for a truer and more scientific interpretation of the data of physical studies."
As Raven reveals 'The Wisdom of God..':
"Is packed with references to and discussions of problems, ranging from the nature of atoms or the influence of the moon upon the tides, to those of the shape of bees' cells, the movements of birds and fishes, the structure of the eye and the growth of the foetus in the womb"

In commenting upon the significance of the 'The Wisdom of God..' Raven states his belief that it did much to convince those of more rigid Christian thinking, that this work was a "Legitimate field for Christian enquiry." This was aided by John's "honest and reverent mind, fearless in facing facts but slow to dogmatise prematurely or to reject established opinion until the evidence was clear."

Reflecting on the attempts of philosophers and scientists throughout time to speculate upon, investigate and validate understanding about ourselves and the universe that we exist in and which surrounds us it is hardly surprising that we have seen the world and ourselves through our own eyes. In short, we have nearly always looked at everything, as we, understandably, still do from our own perspective.

It can be argued that this is another form of survival behaviour. (For example: the importance of stopping and thinking of the consequences before acting in a particular way) However over reliance on this one-eyed view of ourselves and the world, however ingrained and habitual, initially led us to believe that the sun and stars revolved around the earth and that everything revolves around and is subservient to us as human beings. Advances in scientific understanding have led to different conclusions. Yet even those engaged on the frontiers of scientific discovery can still be prone to use arguments that challenge theological belief from an anthropomorphic perspective. We all share these views to a greater or lesser extent . (e.g. our struggle to understand suffering and human disasters as emanating from a caring God while at the same time seeking to explore and acknowledge our desire to be free to choose). Such concerns and perceptions only point to the need for greater understanding and discovery, providing in themselves no conclusive arguments, looked at from our anthropomorphic perspective.

John Hedley Brooke in his paper *'Wise men nowadays think otherwise'*, prepared for the 1999 conference – John Ray and his successors- revealed how John Ray was aware of this anthropomorphic perspective and illustrated how he challenged it in *The wisdom of God,* 1691. As Hedley Brooke noted, Raven, in his 1942 biography of John Ray had argued that in *The Wisdom of God*, Ray had provided what he described as a new Physico-theology: ' Giving appropriate expression to the Christian faith in a scientific age.'

A quotation from *The Wisdom of God* illustrates John Ray's view: "For my part, I cannot believe, that all the things in the world were so made for man, that they have no other use"
And again: "It is generally received opinion that all this visible world was created for man, that man is the end of creation, as if there were no other end of any creating but some way or other to be serviceable to man...but though this be vulgarly received, yet wise men now think otherwise".

In this quotation one sees the extent and breadth of John Ray's thinking providing further evidence of his advanced scholarship.

Part Five
The Seventeenth Century

John Ray lived for nearly all of his life in the seventeenth century. The circumstances and environment that surrounded him were significantly different from those of our own times. It is instructive to list those aspects of our lives that we take for granted and which had no existence in the seventeenth century.

There were no cars, trains or planes for travel, not even the humble bicycle. Work, for the majority of the population, was predominantly agricultural. There were very few large towns. In the middle of the century the population of London was just over 500,000. The next biggest towns were Newcastle, Bristol and Norwich, which had populations of barely 25,000 each. The population of London was bigger than the combined populations of the next fifty towns in England combined.

Life expectancy in the early part of the century was about 40 years, mostly due to the high rate of infant mortality that was between 12 and 13 per cent in the first twelve months of life. However these figures varied considerably between the country and the towns. In London, which probably showed the greatest variations, it depended on whether you lived in wealthy or poor area. For example, in the parish of St Mary's, in the middle of the century, life expectancy was as low as 21 whereas in the more wealthy St Peter's parish the figure was 34-36 years. However, the picture that might be conjured up in the mind of the majority of people dying at such young ages is a mistaken one. If you survived to the age of thirty you could expect to live to the age of 59.

Our current twenty-first century life expectancy of 77 years compared to that of only 47 by 1901 reflects not only major advances in medicine, public hygiene, health and housing but also advances related to modern economic development and significant improvements in family income. The extension of the franchise in the twentieth century also meant that higher social expectations and demands could no longer be ignored by political parties and governments.

Returning to the seventeenth century, the movement of the population from the place of their birth was minimal compared to today. The majority of those moving away from the parish of their birth usually lived in a nearby parish, the move usually dictated by the availability of work. Those who travelled further afar were also predominantly seeking work because of the absence of it in the area where they previously resided.

Homes did not have inside toilets. There was no electricity or gas to provide lighting, heating or cooking. There was therefore no radio or television. There were no computers or typewriters; the quill pen was the main means of writing letters or books and, when it was dark, by the light of a candle.

There were no supermarkets and it was only by 1690 that most towns had shops. The price of food was expensive compared with today. The range of products for sale were equally of a limited nature and much of what was eaten or worn was prepared in the home. This would also include many of the furnishings.

There was no formal Education system or Health Service. Each community sought to provide for its own as best it could.

A person's position in life was, for the vast majority of the population, established through the circumstance of their birth with extremely limited opportunities for moving 'up the ladder.' Improvement was possible for a few if there was evidence of significant ability combined with the good fortune of being noticed by those who were in a position to help and were motivated to do so. This was the favourable position John Ray found himself in as the son of a village Blacksmith and local Herbalist.

Information about what was happening in the world would be passed predominantly by the spoken word, person to person, or in letters. However relatively few people would have been able to read other than those who had had the privilege of an education.

These are a few of the profound differences between our lives and those who lived throughout the seventeenth century. So what was the seventeenth century really like and what were the influences and pressures that John Ray lived through following his birth in 1627?

In Part One – *Life and Times* some of these factors and pressures have been referred to within the context of John Ray's story. It is perhaps helpful now to take a wider view of those major changes that were taking place in seventeenth century society that will allow the reader to reflect further on the background to his life's work and achievements.

Population

The population of England, throughout the period of John Ray's life varied between just over 4 and 5.3 million people, increasing in the first part of the century, falling back and then starting to rise again. It has been suggested that the falling back in population growth was directly related to late marriages within all social groups. This was almost certainly connected to the need and convention of young people to save enough money to be able to set themselves up as an independent household. There was no provision of unemployment or other welfare benefits to save them should they fall on hard times.

Late marriage was also probably linked to the relationship between population growth and price inflation caused by the inability of agricultural production to meet the food resources required, particularly in the first half of the century. In the period between 1500 and 1640, when John Ray was in his thirteenth year, food prices had risen eightfold while wages less than threefold. A majority of the population had to buy much of their food and therefore such purchases formed an increasingly significant part of family expenditure.

Although, as we shall see, the prospects of the nation prospered during the seventeenth century, for the increasing proportion of the nation who were dependant upon wages the century resulted in a decline in living standards. In consequence many thousands of families found it difficult to balance their family budgets and a crisis would beset them should illness or disability arise. As mentioned previously there was no State Benefit system to rescue them if calamity struck.

The decline in the population in the late seventeenth century eased these problems combined with greater agricultural efficiency. As an example, after 1670 England ceased to be a net importer of grain and became an exporter.

While the social movements of people were limited and within a relatively small geographical area, predominantly linked to employment opportunities, the seventeenth century was probably the first century when more people emigrated than came into the country. Those who left were mainly young adults travelling to the New World in the hope of new beginnings, religious freedom or to make their fortune. This movement of people reached its peak in the 1650's and 60's, invariably associated with the effects of the Civil War and religious dissent.

In the seventeenth century England had no standing army, no police force and even the special Regiments of Guards to protect the monarch were only created at the time of the Restoration in the 1660's. It is estimated that after 1660 there were about 3,000 armed men on permanent duty in England with rather more in Ireland and in Tangiers and several thousands with the Dutch and Portuguese armies that could be recalled if necessary.

All this was in complete contrast to the period of the Civil War, when in 1643-4 there were possibly 150,000 men in arms dwindling to less than 25,000 by the late 1640's. For the remainder of the century Local Gentry families formed Militias which were the first line of defence.

It is difficult today to appreciate that in the seventeenth century, with no police force, criminal trials could only take place as a result of accusations made by victims to local Justices of the Peace. Local farmers or craftsmen acted as village constables, taking their turn for twelve-month periods. However, at the beginning of the seventeenth century Church Courts remained powerful in all spheres of life and all English men and women were deemed to be members of the state church. Dissent was a punishable offence and heretics were still burnt at the stake. Nevertheless, by the end of the century Protestant dissent was legally tolerated and Church Courts were to lose nearly all their functions.

Having regard to the independence of Justices of the Peace, during the reign of the early Stuarts, they were subject to direction from Whitehall with accountability for disobedience exercised through the Star Chamber. The Star Chamber had originally been set up as a Court of the King's Council in Medieval England meeting in the Star Chamber of Westminster Palace. Its misuse by Charles I to enforce unpopular policies led to its abolition in 1641 by Parliament, the year before the start of the Civil War. By the early years of the 1700's Country Gentlemen and their tight knit oligarchies were effectively the local Government of the country answerable only to people like themselves in parliament.

Throughout the seventeenth century, Government, significantly smaller and different from today, was practised by a ritual of consent. This was exercised centrally by parliament and applied in the country by selected Gentry, some 3,000 in the early part of the century rising to 5,000 by the end, all chosen by the Crown, save during the ten-year Rule of Oliver Cromwell in the middle of the century. This ritual of consent involved the process of persuading those who ruled the town and country that it was in their mutual interest to agree to what was proposed.

The relaxation of central government control over local areas after the 1660's increased the stature of the Lord Lieutenant and made country society even more hierarchical. It is therefore no surprise that it was the House Of Lords that was the most effective wing of parliament providing the first and sustained challenge to the reign of James II in 1685, leading to his exile and the enthronement by parliament of William III in 1689. However, the fundamental change from belief in the Divine Right of Kings and its associated powers, espoused by James I (1603-1625) to the control of the monarchy by parliament was in effect the control of the monarchy by the aristocracy, acting in parliament.

Economic Progress and Taxation for the needs of effective government

Put simply in the absence of any effective system of taxation other than by raising revenue from the land, the governments of Stuart England had insufficient financial resources to carry out the rising expectations of their people. The main engine of change in the seventeenth century was probably economic progress rather than the serious consequences of religious disputes, conducted from the pulpit and the printed word, or the political disputes between the monarch and parliament that straddled the century.

Argument,nonetheless, provided the lifeblood of society, embracing issues of taxation, liberty, land, trade, authority and property. What this maelstrom of argument helped create in concert with increased economic efficiency was the emergence of England, a second class power at the start of the century, into the leading world power by the early 1700's, as the dominant geographical part of a unified Great Britain.

In consequence, Britain became one of the wealthiest nations of the world with an expanding maritime and colonial empire. The boom time began in the 1670's with an expansion in trade that has been called the 'Commercial

Revolution' leading to the setting up of the Bank of England in 1694, which became one of the chief financial centres of the world. The Toleration Act of 1689 allowed dissenters and Roman Catholics freedom from the established church and such a relaxation may well have contributed to the an increased concentration of time, creative energy and enterprise into economic and trade interests and less into sectarian anxieties and strategies for survival.

We can now add to this introduction to the seventeenth century and the gathering momentum of Great Britain as a world Empire, those essential ingredients that were directly linked to John Ray's life and personal experience, forming the background or stage upon which he set forth on his life's work.

England's intellectual ascendancy, developed throughout the seventeenth century, was a tribute to changes in thinking and the preparedness to embrace new interpretations and explanations for the natural world rather than rely on superstitious or untested beliefs. Isaac Newton's famous comment:

"If I have seen further it is by standing on the shoulders of giants" is both an acknowledgement of predecessors and an insight into the processes of understanding and development. The scientific achievements of the century were primarily those arising from accurate observation rather than book learning. Again Isaac Newton put his finger on this with his comment:

"Plato is my friend, Aristotle is my friend but my best friend is truth"

Mark Kishlansky in his book *A Monarchy Transformed 1603-1714* summed up the changes that had occurred in the seventeenth century and talked about the birth of the modern business world, science coming of age, the withering of feudal practices, the founding of great merchant companies trading in the East Indies and in Africa. In support and forming an integral part of this development were the founding of the Bank of England and the Bank of Scotland with the introduction of cheques, banknotes and milled coins, making possible an economy based on money. This was followed by the creation of the Stock Exchange and the facility of having a national debt that, in turn, made possible an economy based on credit. Excise and land tax reshaped Government finance. Insurance Companies were born.

Conditions in Essex

In his book, *Essex In History* Kenneth Neale argues that following the death of Elizabeth I, in 1603, the aspirations and actions of the Stuart Kings were incompatible with the growth of parliamentary authority. This was particularly the case in respect of James I, Charles I and James II.

Within Essex, together with others of their class in the surrounding counties, the Gentry were resistant to the Crown when it attempted to threaten their independence. Therefore because of their penury the autocratic attempts by Stuart kings to raise finances for ventures, not acceptable to the gentry of parliament or those in the country, were both foolish and dangerous.

In particular the revolt by the Scots to Charles I attempt to reinstate bishops into the Scottish church destroyed the legitimacy of his rule and in 1639 the lucrative source of his income through 'Ship money' virtually dried up. In Essex, in 1638 only £1,052 of the £26,750 demanded was not collected but in the following year only £331 was collected of the £8,000 assessed. Ship money had been a tax raised by the monarch in times of emergency for the defence of the coast. Under Charles I it gained notoriety when he levied it indiscriminently between 1634 and 1639.

Attempts to raise a force from Essex against the Calvinist Scots resulted in what has been described as a fiasco. Essex was charged with raising some £2,400 for the army but barely a quarter was raised.

As far as the effects of the Civil War are concerned the Essex Gentry were split in their loyalties although the strength of puritan feeling in the county was more sympathetic to parliament than the monarch. Essex was also part of the Eastern Association of areas providing support to Oliver Cromwell who looked to the county for resources and men for his Model Army. Cromwell's wife was an Essex lady from Felsted, daughter of Sir Jame Bourchier.

As in the country as a whole, so also in Essex, the parliamentary army was to prove successful because it was better equipped, more mobile and more effectively led than those who joined together to fight for the king. However, notwithstanding its commitment to the parliamentary cause, Essex did not become involved in hostilities until the Siege of Colchester in 1648.

It will assist if we also realise the difference in population between the Essex we know today and the Essex of the seventeenth century. William Hunt in his book, *The Puritan Movement,* 1983, states that the population of Essex at the Death of Queen Elizabeth I, in 1603, was 100,000. The only town of any significant size was that of Colchester with a population nearing 9,000 and the nearest to that were the combined clothing communities of Braintree and Bocking with 2,500. No other town contained as many as 2,000. The third largest community was Coggeshall. Chelmsford, Saffron Walden and Dunmow, as market towns, followed in Coggeshall's wake. By 1670 the population of Essex had expanded to 170,000.

However, as an indication of the devastating impact of the plague in Essex on family, community and employment, the following mortality figures indicate the extent of the catastrophe. The three communities most badly affected were Colchester, where in the sixteen months between August 1665 and December 1666 some 5,000 people died, all but 500 being attributed to the plague, almost half of the population. In Braintree 665 people died of the plague in 1666, more than a third of the population and in the same year, in Bocking, 423. It is speculated that the reason why they were so badly affected may have been because they were all growing textile communities, probably with younger populations, living in overcrowded and insanitary conditions.

They also had large numbers of poor workers in spinning and weaving who would have seen their livings collapse as the plague spread.

John Ray returned to Essex from his continental tour in the early part of 1666 and in June he travelled to Cambridge, so he would have been fully appraised of the seriousness of conditions and must have been fearful for his own and his family's well being.

The effects of the Civil War and Religious conflicts upon John Ray

It is interesting to speculate upon the effects of the Civil War on John Ray and his family. The period, including the rule of Oliver Cromwell (1649-1658) and the short period when his son Richard ruled before the Restoration of Charles II in 1660, encompassed twenty years of John Ray's life. At the start of the troubles he would have been about thirteen and at the Restoration he was thirty-two years old. Given his rise to eminence within Cambridge it would have been impossible for him not to be influenced by such calamitous and challenging events.

Survival, in terms of his position at the university would have required a level of diplomacy and tact because of the implications of being identified with either cause, given the political fissures and pressures that existed.

As we have previously stated, Raven identified Ray within the Puritan tradition and therefore, at first sight, if this is the case, more likely to have been identified with the parliamentary cause. However the work of Susan McMahon, specifically in her paper *"In these times of giddiness and distraction"*, 1999, challenges Raven's assertion. She argues persuasively that John Ray's beliefs and religious practices were essentially those of someone in support of the established church. As he identified himself:

" A true though unworthy Son of the Church by law established in this kingdom"

Her rationale is based on his associates and friends, many of whom were Anglicans who became clergymen and bishops within the established church.

Additionally following his refusal to sign the oath disavowing the covenant in 1662 and his resultant loss of office at the university and as a Clergyman, had John been perceived solely as a puritan then he would never have retained such friendships. Neither would he have, as Susan McMahon argues, established his reputation in producing a model of natural history, which provided an understanding of the natural world as a legitimate expression of religious thinking and worship.

As far as John Ray's political affiliations are concerned his presence at Trinity, during the period from his entering Cambridge at the age of 16, in 1644, until his resignation in 1662 when he was 34, suggests that he was seen as a loyal supporter of the established church. Additionally that he was able to transcend the political debate and pressures to ensure his survival until he chose to take matters into his own hands by his resignation.

A third explanation indicates why he was able to transcend the religious divide. Put simply John Ray's beliefs straddled both those of the established church and the dissenting tradition and, in consequence, he gained respect from both sides. This argument was contained in a paper by Colin Price, *John Ray's Wisdom of God in the Dissenting Tradition* also produced at the 1999 Conference 'John Ray and his Successors'

Why he was able to successfully straddle this seemingly impossible divide and earn the respect of both sides is probably linked to those major structural changes that were taking place within the seventeenth century with regard to religious practice and church affiliation.

In summary the Interregnum presided over by Oliver Cromwell and his son (1649-1660) resulted in the ending of the established English Episcopal Church with its requirement of conformity backed by the force of law. This was followed by the introduction of Presbyterianism. (In effect the abolition of Bishops in favour of Church Elders). Cathedrals were turned into preaching centres, used as barracks or even prisons.

However, at the Restoration, from the time when Charles II became King in 1660, the Episcopal Church of Bishops was reinstated and in 1662 the Act of Uniformity attempted to put back in place what had existed previously since 1559. Rather than attempt to find an inclusive solution to religious worship uniformity was re-imposed.

Such an imposition created a short-term crisis and the ejection of some 2000 clerics and teachers. However the changes brought about by Cromwell during the Interregnum had a profound effect upon Dissenters who had formed themselves into numerous sects, churches and gatherings including the Baptists and Quakers, both of whom were to play a leading role and have significant influence.

Hitherto, the religious uniformity imposed in 1559, which lasted up to 1649 eventually resulted in what amounted to a 'wait and see' approach by many Puritan dissenters who were prepared to tolerate the status quo, presumably in the hope that the situation would eventually improve. The experience of greater freedom during the Interregnum (1649-1660) was to change their disposition to that of not being prepared to wait and to actively seek the proliferation of their religious practices by clear separation from the established church.

Therefore the Act of Uniformity in 1662 galvanised the Dissenters and provided a trigger for consolidating separate development, which was then legally accepted and recognised by The Toleration Act of 1689.

In effect, what was happening, from the time when John Ray was in his early twenties and for the remainder of his life, was that the powers of the established church were in decline and the freedom to dissent was becoming more entrenched. These dynamic and seismic changes probably explain why his personal beliefs and approach to his work was accepted by both traditions and facilitated respect from both.

Raven's assertion that John Ray was essentially a puritan may have originated from, or be explained by, the simplicity with which John approached the practice of his faith and his dislike of ritual and the taking of oaths. Additionally, his disdain for emotional argument bereft of logical thought. However, as we have seen it was possible for a person of prudent disposition to accept significant parts of the established church and retain a dissenting view that could be respected.

Perhaps what John Ray epitomised most of all to his friends, and which made him such a clear supporter of the established church was that his model of natural science was perceived to be in keeping with the development of Anglican thinking in the seventeenth century. This thinking included the realisation that it had to become more tolerant, prepared to change and look afresh at the world.

Yet when one compares the underlying principles of Puritan science, as set out in Colin Price's 1999 paper it is easy to see how close they were to John Ray's own beliefs. They included *'the complete acceptance that the world is God's; that it is in all essence mysterious and awesome and it is wholly beyond the capacity of Man to totally comprehend; yet we are by the grace of God given to understand; but in understanding we are not discovering the nature of Nature but the nature of God or of some minute aspect of His own Glory of which we are participating...'*

Given these two positions from the established and dissenting traditions it is clear that John Ray was not only a man of his times but his ideas and opinions relating to scientific development, set within his religious beliefs, ensured he played an enabling role in both scientific and religious thinking.

Part Six
John Ray's Legacy

The economic, social and scientific developments of the seventeenth century provided the catalysts for future progress. Through his life's work, John Ray can also be truly regarded as the catalyst for significant advances in the natural sciences, his abilities and values particularly matched to the needs of his times.

Susan McMahon, in her 2001 thesis: *Constructing Natural History in England 1650-1700,* argued that John Ray's legacy: "was to build an enduring foundation for the discipline of natural history as a legitimate enterprise for structuring and interpreting nature." She goes on to state how his natural theology was, effectively, the practical application of natural history as a means of understanding God and his creation of the world. The specific undertaking of such work known as natural philosophy

It is one of the principal contentions of this book that his work consolidated the achievements of his predecessors, and laid the foundations for those who were to follow him both in relation to the content, methods, underlying principles and values of his work

In particular, he effectively dealt with the duplications and confusions he found in the work of his predecessors through his systematic and orderly methods, fully realising that to move forward required what we might describe today as an effective stocktaking and auditing exercise. We need to reflect on the personal and professional discipline required for such extensive work with so few tools at his disposal. No information technology to help him access, revise, re-order, print or store his information as we have today. His work required the laborious task of writing everything down by hand and the need to locate and read relevant material from predecessors and contemporaries so easily available today on the Internet.

The legacy that John Ray has handed down to us includes the honesty with which he approached his work. His recognition that it was not always possible to complete his work to the standard he would have wished either because he did not have access to other sources of information or because of time constraints imposed upon him by others seeking his help. Then there was his recognition that what was known and could be discovered in his lifetime was also limited and that further progress would inevitably follow after his death.

This is the desired level of humility required by scientists. It provides a sense of proportion within the context of specific scientific scholarship and achievement, ensuring, particularly for those who have success, that they remain aware of and constructively responsive to the challenges of colleagues, facilitating progress both in themselves and their work.

Such an approach, exemplified by John Ray, reveals the level of integrity that is an integral part of any genuine scientific endeavour. His life's work is a model for those who wish to follow in his footsteps; in particular the importance of understanding what has gone before, of sorting out that which is confusing or repetitive, of bringing a sense of order and systematic planning to the task in hand. Put simply he exemplified the need to have thought through and developed a relevant and appropriate conceptual framework for a project that is also measurable and therefore credible. The model he hands down to us also includes a mind that is open to surprises, learning, difference, enquiry, challenge and other people's perspectives. All of these qualities are the indispensable requirements of a scientific mind.

The industriousness, prodigious output and excellence of his scholarship and the wide range and extent of his work in the natural sciences clearly impressed, inspired and motivated many of his contemporaries and those who succeeded him. It is an example that perhaps few can attain but everyone can aspire to and exists as an incentive to us all in present times. This is especially relevant given the advantages we have with the use of and access to modern technology especially in respect of information gathering and communication.

Perhaps another motivational trigger for us might be in reflecting on the enthusiasm John Ray had for the study of the natural world and how he saw it as his purpose to do all he could to advance understanding. Here one can see how he made the use of his time subordinate to his perceived duty.

Inherent in his approach to all his scientific endeavours was the need for verification first and foremost. Opinions are legion but convincing evidence is the credible tool for earning respect among contemporaries and those who follow. In arriving at a verifiable position it is essential, as he emphasised, to make meticulous notes and accurate descriptions of any subject to be studied or experiment to be undertaken. Such an approach requires a level of personal discipline so amply illustrated in his life's work and in particular for the last twenty-five years of his life when his health was failing and when he was both a husband and the father of four daughters.

Notwithstanding all the work undertaken by John Ray so far described in this book there is yet more that he is renowned for, directly related to his flair for languages. Raven has argued that his interest in dialect and proverbs was associated with his love of words, their derivation and meanings. Additionally that his choice in their study and in his publications of his *Collection of English Proverbs,* 1670, and *Collection of English words,* 1673, may well have been linked to his coming from a rural background into a university life predominantly populated by those of significant means and high social status.

Raven argues that this aspect of his work is possibly an illustration of how he responded to the challenges he faced as a poor scholar with all the probable difficulties of mixing with those of high birth combined with the social esteem of his academic successes.

As Raven concludes, what was so characteristic of John Ray was how he accepted his position in life without aggressiveness or subservience. This is clearly the mark of a person who is at ease with himself, combining a finely balanced degree of self-confident assertiveness and humility; a legacy we can all aspire to achieve in our own lives.

In seeking to find the clue to the array of personal and professional qualities he presented to the world he would always return to his belief in God and how he felt his work was to bring to a wider audience the beauty and diversity of Divine Creation. If it were asked what is John Ray's abiding legacy to the world it is probably the importance of the vital relationship between his beliefs, his work and the way he lived his life.

His contribution to the natural sciences was and will remain of major significance but all this would probably not have seen the light of day had it not been for his belief in God handed down to him by his parents and adopted as his own.

Right: The John Ray Garden within the Braintree & Bocking Public Gardens, Braintree

Left: The John Ray Statue, designed by Faith Winter stands outside the Braintree District Museum.

Above: Black Notley church and farm photographed from the John Ray walk. A nine-mile walk beginning and ending at Braintree and Witham stations.

Above: A small woodland along the John Ray walk at White Notley Green.
Below: The walk passes close to the village of White Notley viewed here across the fields

CATALOGUS
PLANTARUM
CIRCA
CANTABRIGIAM
nascentium:

In qua exhibentur
Quotquot hactenus inventæ sunt, quæ
vel sponte proveniunt, vel in
agris feruntur;

Unà cum
Synonymis selectioribus, locis natalibus
& observationibus quibusdam
oppidò raris.

Adjiciuntur in gratiam tyronum,
Index Anglo-latinus, Index locorum,
Etymologia nominum, & Explicatio
quorundam terminorum.

CANTABRIGIÆ:
Excudebat *Joann. Field*, celeberrimæ
Academiæ Typographus.
Impensis Gulielmi Nealand, *Bibliopola.*
Ann. Dom. 1660.

Left: Frontispiece from Ray's *Cambridge Catalogue [Catalogus Plantarum circa Cantabrigiam nascentium)*

Right: Frontispiece from Ray's *English Catalogue. Catalogus Plantarum Angliae*

CATALOGUS
PLANTARUM
ANGLIÆ,
ET
INSULARUM Adjacentium:
Tùm Indigenas, tum in agris pas-
sim cultas complectens.

In quo præter Synonyma necessaria
facultates quoque summatim tra-
duntur, unà cum Observationibus
& Experimentis Novis Medicis &
Physicis.

OPERA
JOANNIS RAII M. A.
& Societatis Regiæ Sodalis.

LONDINI,
Typis E. C. & A. C. Impensis *J. Martyn,* Regalis So-
cietatis Typographi, ad Insigne Campanæ in
Cœmeterio D. Pauli. MDCLXX.

Illustrations from Willughby's *Ornithology*

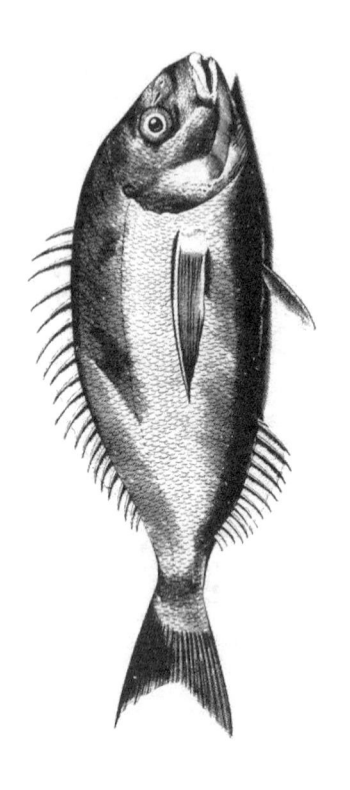

Left: Samuel Pepys paid for many of the illustrations in Willughby's *Historia Piscium*. This fish is one of the illustrations.

Right: Veronica spicata. An illustration taken from Ray's *Flora of Britain*

This bust of Ray by Roubiliac is in the Wren Library at Trinity College Cambridge

Left: The Purple Emperor Butterfly. This butterfly was a common visitor to the woods around Black Notley. Ray described forty-seven British butterflies.

Right: Burnished Brass moth. Specimens were caught by Ray's daughters in the garden at Dewlands.

Left: The Robin Redbreast observed by Ray as eating hairless caterpillars and avoiding hairy specimens

Glossary

Alchemy: the medieval form of chemistry concerned with trying to change base metals into gold and to find an elixir to prolong life indefinitely.
Anatomy: the study of the physical structure of animals and plants.
Anglican: a member of the Church of England.
Anthropocentric: regarding the human being as the most important factor in the universe.
Anthropology: the study of human origins, institutions and beliefs.
Anthropomorphism: the attribution of human form or personality to a God, animal or object.
Apothecary: A chemist.
Astrology: the study of the alleged influence of the stars, planets, sun and moon on human affairs.
Astronomy: the study of celestial bodies and the universe of which they are a part.
Biology: the study of living organisms including their form (Morphology), physiology, behaviour, origin and distribution.
Botany: the scientific study of plants.
Calyx: the outer leaves that protect the developing bud of a flower.
Dicotyledons: the larger of the two main groups of flowering plants that include hardwood trees, shrubs and many herbaceous plants. Characterised by having two seed leaves. (see also Monocotyledons).
Episcopacy: government of a church by Bishops.
Etymology: the study of the sources and development of words.
Gentry: old-fashioned term referring to people just below the nobility in social status.
Geocentric: Having the earth as the centre.
Geometric system: as advanced by the ancient Greek scholars, known as the Ptolemaic system, where it was

believed that the Moon, Mercury, Venus, Sun, Mars, Jupiter, and Saturn moved around the earth.
Heliocentric: any model of the solar system in which the planets move around the sun.
Monocotyledons: the smaller of the two main groups of flowering plants including palms, bananas, orchids, grasses, lilies, daffodils, irises, tulips, crocuses. They are characterised by having a single seed leaf. (cotyledon).
Morphology: the study of the forms and structures of organisms.
Natural Theology: the attempt to find knowledge of God through the use of reason and the observation and study of the world.
Ornithology: the study of birds.
Ontology: the branch of philosophy that deals with the theory of being and considers questions of what is and what is not.
Paleontology: the study of ancient organisms from their fossil remains in rock.
Petal: the brightly coloured parts of flowers that form the head of the flower.
Pharmacology: the study of drugs.
Philosophy: the study of knowledge, thought and the meaning of life.
Physiology: the study of the functioning of organisms.
Presbyterian: designating church government by lay elders.
Presbyterianism: A protestant church based on government by elders, comprising ministers and laymen all having equal rank. Originated with the 16th Century followers of Calvin in Scotland. In Scotland its tenets were formulated by John Knox (1514-1572) and it became the established church.
Protestant: follower of any of the Christian churches that separated from the Roman Catholic Church in the 16th century.
Ptolemaic system: as advanced by ancient Greek scholars where it was believed that the Moon, Mercury, Venus, Sun, Mars, Jupiter and Saturn moved around the Earth.

Puritan: a member of the English Protestant church who wished to remove from the Church of England most of its rituals and hierarchy which were reminiscent of Roman Catholicism. Puritans became associated with the Parliamentarians in the Civil War.

Renaissance: the revival of classical art, literature and learning in Europe in the 14th, 15th and 16th centuries.

Royal Society: the oldest and most important scientific society in the UK, originating in 1645 and incorporated by royal charter in 1662.

Science: the study of the nature and behaviour of the physical universe based on observation, experiment and measurement.

Squire: country gentleman in England, mainly the main landowner in a local community.

Taxonomy: the branch of biology concerned with the classification of plants and animals into groups based on their similarities and differences.

Teleology: the doctrine that there is evidence of purpose or design in the universe. As applied in Biology: that natural phenomena have a pre-determined purpose and are not determined by mechanical laws.

Theology: the systematic study of religions and religious beliefs.

Transpiration: the loss of water vapour from the surface of a plant, which occurs mainly through small pores (stomata) in the leaves.

Zoology: the study of animals including their classification, anatomy, physiology, history and habits.

Biographical details

Aldrovandi, Ulysses. (1522-1605). Bolognese botanist and naturalist who carried out extensive work on plant classification.

Allen, Benjamin. (1663-1738) Physician and amateur naturalist. Doctor to John Ray and his family until 1698 when they became estranged, following the death of their daughter, Mary. A pupil of St Paul's School before entering Queen's College, Cambridge, in 1681. In 1690 he treated John Ray for pneumonia and the Ray's youngest daughter, 'Jenny' (Jane), for what he described as epilepsy, probably infantile convulsions.

Joined the practice of Joshua Draper in Braintree and married his daughter, Katherine Draper. John Ray had formed a high opinion of his abilities especially following his discovery of the male Glow-worm and of the Death-watch Beetle.

John Ray's wife, Margaret, became Godparent to his eldest son, Thomas, in 1697. Clearly had a great admiration for John Ray, notwithstanding their estrangement in 1698, as he chose a grave next to Ray's in Black Notley Churchyard.

Anselm, St (1033-1109) Italian theologian and philosopher. A leading early scholastic philosopher famous for his formulation that God is "That than which nothing greater can be conceived." Appointed Archbishop of Canterbury in 1093.

Aristotle, (384-322 BC) Greek philosopher and scientist who joined Plato's academy. Wrote over 400 books on different aspects of learning including ethics, biology, physics, and psychology.

Ashmole, Elias. (1617-1692). Born in Staffordshire. His work on Alchemy set out in his publication *Theatrum Chymicum Britannicum* brought together previously unpublished manuscripts by English Chemists. He later moved to South London lodging with the collector and gardener, John Tradescant who had put together great collections including plants, minerals and coins. These he left to Elias Ashmole in his will. Famous for the museum that bears his name in Oxford. His collections were donated to Oxford in 1675 and put on Public display from 1683.

Bacon, Francis. (1561-1626) Lawyer and philosopher who had a major influence on scientific thinking in the 17th century. His *The Advancement of Learning* in 1605 presented a new classification of sciences. In subsequent works he argued that knowledge could be derived only from experience advocating the scientific method of induction.

Barrow, Isaac. (1630-1677). Mathematician and Theologian. Close friend of John Ray at Cambridge. Described by Raven as a man of great and varied learning and a pioneer in the development of Differential Calculus (Calculus: Mathematical techniques based on the concept of infinitely small changes in continuously varying quantities. Differential Calculus: The system of rules for making such calculations). In 1663 Barrow became the first Lucasian Professor of Mathematics at Cambridge. The Lucasian chair was the gift of Sir Henry Lucas MP. Barrow subsequently became Master of Trinity College. Also developed a popular reputation through his preaching.

Bauhin, Gaspard. (1560-1624) brother of Jean whose publication *Pinax Theatri Botanici* helped reduce the confusion of the many different names that had been given to plants by producing a nomenclature that both included a generic and a specific name.

Bauhin, Jean. (1541-1605) Elder brother of Gaspard. French doctor who studied botany. Major work: *Historia Plantarum universalis* published after his death; the most extensive work on botany up to that time.

Boyle, Robert. (1627-1691) Irish physicist and chemist who demonstrated that the air possesses weight and is necessary for the transition of sound. His work in chemistry distinguished elements, compounds and mixtures and his work on gases produced what is known as Boyle's law indicating that at a constant temperature the pressure of a unit mass of gas is inversely proportional to its volume.

Buffon, Georges Louis Leclerc. (1707-1788) French naturalist who formulated a theory of evolution estimating that the earth might be 75,000 years old, with man appearing at 40,000 years, challenging biblical interpretations of the earth's age.

Bullock, Edward. Friend of John Ray who lent him his home, Faulkbourne Hall, near Witham, Essex, in 1677. John Ray and his wife lived there for nearly two years. John Ray had been tutor to Bullock's son, Edward, who later treated John and his family with coolness. This was possibly because he had married Josiah Child's daughter, May. Child had married Emma Willughby following the death of her husband Francis and she disapproved of John Ray.

Cesalpino, Andrea (1519-1603). An Italian who made significant early advances in the classification of plants and yet who acknowledged his debt to the Greek botanist, Theophrastus whose work preceded that of Cesalpino's by some 1700 years. Cesalpino's major publication in 1583 was *De Platis libri XV1* that included fifteen books containing a description of some 1,500 plants.

Charles I (1600-1649) King of England, Scotland and Ireland who succeeded his father, James I, in 1625. His stubborn and tactless behaviour exemplified in his attempting to impose Bishops on the Scottish Church and his evident lack of judgement were fatal flaws in his personality. His dependency on parliament for raising money led to acrimonious disputes that eventually resulted in the Civil War and his execution in 1649.

Charles II (1630-1685) Second son of Charles I. Succeeded to the throne in 1660 at the Restoration of the monarchy following the rule of Oliver Cromwell and his son, Richard Cromwell. A great patron of the Arts he was also described as 'The merry Monarch.' Said to be intelligent, tolerant and interested in scientific development. His Catholic sympathies are said to have aroused suspicion associated with his secret treaties with France through which he tried to raise money denied him by parliament. Money given him by King Louis XIV was on condition that he

returned England to the Roman Catholic Church. His Reign also witnessed the great human tragedies of the Great Plague, 1664-1666, which killed over 65,000 people in the south east of England. Additionally, the Great Fire of London, 1666, which destroyed some 13,000 buildings, 89 Churches and 50 Guildhalls yet seemingly less than ten people due to the slow spread of the fire leaving ample time for evacuation. The fire helped put a stop to the plague in London.
Child, Josiah. (1630-1699). Described by Raven in his biography of John Ray as 'notorious but immensely wealthy', the second husband of Emma Willughby. Child rose from an apprentice to victualler of the fleet and Chairman of the East India Company. Member of Parliament.
Clusius, Carolus. (1526-1609). French physician and botanist who studied with Guillaume Rondelet. Also understood eight languages. His first publication was a French translation of Rembert Dodoen's *Herbal* that had been published in Antwerp in 1557. In 1593 he was appointed honorary professor of botany at the University of Leiden.
Collins, Samuel. (c1576-1657) Eminent vicar of St Michael's church, Braintree, during John Ray's education at the Braintree Grammar School, located in what is now the Jesus Chapel of the church. A graduate of Trinity college, Cambridge, (1599-1600) and ordained in Norwich in 1601. Instrumental in ensuring that John Ray benefited from the bequest of a wealthy businessman who left a sum of money for the education of 'poor scholars' at Catherine Hall, Cambridge. Famous for his inauguration of the 'Four and Twenty' one of the earliest forms of local government.
Cromwell, Oliver. (1599-1658) English soldier and Statesman becoming the 'Lord protector of England' 1653-1658. A puritan who became the leader of the Parliamentarians who defeated Charles I in the Civil War and oversaw his execution. An able administrator and commander of soldiers who created 'The Model Army' that was more efficient and better mobilised than the Royalist

troops. Although he established Puritanism throughout the country he was tolerant to other churches save for Catholics in Ireland. Ultimately he failed to find a satisfactory basis for constitutional reform without the monarchy.
Cromwell, Richard. (1626-1712) Son of Oliver Cromwell who succeeded his father in 1658 but who was forced to abdicate in 1660 by the army, leading to the 'Restoration' of Charles II.
Dale, Samuel. (1659-1738). Physician and amateur naturalist who lived in Braintree and was a close friend of John Ray. Described as a man who played an honourable part in the local community. Under John Ray's guidance he travelled widely in East Anglia searching for plants and raised many different species from seed in his garden. John Ray sent him his collection of insects, shortly before his death and Dale was responsible for preparing a catalogue of John Ray's collection of books, after his death. Some 1,500 volumes were sold by auction in London in the March 1708.
Duckfield, Daniel. (d1645). Tutor to John Ray while he was a Catherine Hall, Cambridge. An Essex man who had probably been brought up near Brentwood and who had graduated at Catherine Hall 1635-6, gaining his fellowship the following year. His death in May 1645 is suggested by Raven as one of the reasons that may have influenced John Ray to transfer to Trinity College.
Duport, James. John Ray's tutor at Trinity College Born in Cambridge, his father being Master of Jesus College. He had been at Trinity since 1622 and had gained a great reputation as a scholar and teacher.
Evelyn, John. (1620-1706) English diarist who helped found the Royal Society.
Fibonacci, Leonardo. (c1170-c1230) Italian mathematician who travelled extensively, especially in North Africa, where he learnt the decimal system of numerals. Although publishing the system in Europe it took a long time for it to be accepted.
Gesner, Conrad. (1516-1565) Swiss physician also described as one of the founders of modern zoology and

botany. He completed a survey of animal life *Historiae Animalium* in five volumes and described many species of plants often through woodcut illustrations.

Goad, Thomas. (d1638) Rector of Black Notley Church when John Ray was a boy. His father was provost of Kings College, Cambridge. Thomas was educated at Eton and admitted to a fellowship at Kings and was resident at Cambridge until 1611. He became rector of Black Notley church in 1625. He has been described as a man of versatile mind, intellectual interests and dominating personality. It well may be that he spotted the evident ability of John Ray and was one of those influencing his education.

Hobbes, Thomas. A wealthy businessman of Grays Inn, London, who provided the Scholarship for John Ray to enter Catherine Hall, Cambridge. In his will, dated the 21st February 1631, he bequeathed cottages and lands in Braintree in trust for the payment of £5 a year: 'To the vicar of Braintree and his successors.' This included provision for the maintenance of 'two or three hopeful poor scholars, students in the University of Cambridge, namely in Catherine Hall and Emanuel College.' The will gave the controlling choice in the selection of the pupil to the vicar of Braintree.

James I, (1566-1625). Became James VI of Scotland in 1567 and James I of England, in 1603, the first King to reign over both countries. Has been described as clever and well educated but not popular. He regularly proclaimed the 'Divine Right of Kings' to assert that the King was above the law. He therefore expected parliament to obey him without question but found himself opposed by parliament who denied him money to pay his debts. Overall he appears to have been a man with high ideals but incapable of making effective political relationships and more likely, through his behaviour, to strengthen opposition against him.

James II, (1633-1701) Came to the Throne in 1685 the third son of Charles I and brother of Charles II. His Roman Catholic faith and his period of religious persecution, following the battle at Sedgemoor, with his attempt to replace Protestantism, led to his rapid downfall in what has been described as the 'Glorious Revolution.' In 1689 he was replaced by William III. James spent his remaining days in France.

Johnson, Thomas (circa 1605-1644) London Apothecary, botanist and herbalist who in 1629 produced an account of botanical journeys in Hampstead Heath and Kent where he listed the plants he found. Perhaps one of if not the first book of local flora. His subsequent work on Herbals was known to and used by John Ray who spoke highly of him. Died from wounds sustained in the Civil War.

Jung, Joachim (1587-1657) from Lubeck. Professor of Natural Science at Hamburg. His work was an important source to John Ray because of his interest in the structure of plants and ideas of classification. John Ray acknowledged this in *Historia Plantarum,* in particular, Jung's work on physiology.

Lankester, Edwin. Secretary of the Ray Society founded in 1844 who edited their Publication in 1846 entitled: *Memorials of John Ray.*

Linnaeus, Carl. (1707-1778) Swedish botanist who significantly developed John Ray's system of plant classification and produced his own system of naming plants which bears his name. This provided a generic then specific name for each plant. He grouped related genera into classes and combined related classes into orders. He published *Systema Naturae* in 1735, *Genera Plantarum* in 1737 and *Species plantarum* in 1753. Often called the Father of Taxonomy, his ideas influenced generations of biologists.

Mouffet, Thomas. (d1604) His *Insectorum Theatrum* was not published until 1634 but was considered a work of merit, notwithstanding inaccuracies, which John Ray used when undertaking his own studies on insects.

Muller, Johannes. German astronomer in the fifteenth century.

Newton, Isaac. (1642-1727) British physicist and mathematician. A professor at Cambridge (1669-1701) famous for his discovery of gravity. President of the Royal Society from 1703 until his death. Einstein is quoted as

saying of him "In one person he combined the experimenter, the theorist, the mechanic, not least the artist in exposition."
Oakley, John. From Launton near Bicester, Oxfordshire. Father of Margaret Oakley, John Ray's wife.
Oakley, Margaret. Governess to Francis and Emma Willughby's children. Became John Ray's wife on the 5th June 1673 when she was aged twenty and John Ray forty-five. They were married in Middleton Church, Warwickshire.
Parkinson, John (1567-1650). Herbalist. Botanist to Charles I. His work *Theatricum Boticum* published in 1640 claimed to include all the known plants save those he had included in his earlier work *Paradisi in Sole Paridisus terrestris* (first published in 1629). John Ray used Parkinson's second book as one of the many sources of his work on plants.
Pepys, Samuel (1633-1703) English Diarist covering the period 1658-1669. His diary included descriptions of the Restoration of Charles II, the effects of the plague and the Fire of London, illustrating his keen interest in the details of 17th Century life. Member of Parliament (1673 –1687) and President of the Royal Society (1684-1686). In 1685 he paid £50, towards the cost of 79 illustrative plates, for John Ray's *History of Fishes,* encouraging other members of the Royal Society to pay for additional plates to ensure the book was published.
Plato, (429-347BC) Greek philosopher and a devoted follower of Socrates. Following Socrates' death and after many years of travel he returned to Athens and founded his famous academy to which he devoted the rest of his life.
Plume, Joseph. (d1686). Succeeded Thomas Goad on the 13th August 1638, as rector of Black Notley church. Originated from Suffolk, graduated from Queen's college, Cambridge, in 1625-6, made fellow in 1629 and ordained the following year. Raven considers that he had a significant influence in advancing John Ray's education.

Purbach, George von. (1423-1461). German astronomer.
Ray, Catherine. (Daughter of John Ray) Born 3rd April 1687. Married Thomas Beadle of Billericay, who was a farmer.
Ray, Elizabeth. (c1600-1679).Mother of John Ray. Herbalist in Black Notley treating those who were sick with medicinal remedies from plants. Introduced John to the beauty of nature and her religious beliefs, which became his own.
Ray, Elizabeth. (Sister of John Ray) Born 1625.
Ray, Jane. Youngest daughter of John Ray, born on the 10th February 1689. Married the Rev. Joshua Blower, Vicar of Bradwell near Coggeshall.
Ray, Margaret. (Daughter of John Ray) Born 12th August 1684. Twin sister of Mary. Married John Thomas, of Langford.
Ray, Mary. (Daughter of John Ray) Born 12th August 1684. Died on 29th January 1698 in her fourteenth year. Twin sister of Margaret.
Ray, Roger. (1594-1656). Father of John Ray. Blacksmith in Black Notley. Influenced John's thinking about the importance of and relationship between structure and function through John's observation of his work as a skilled craftsman.
Ray, Roger (1624-1632). Brother of John Ray. Died of Smallpox aged eight.
Robinson, Tancred. (d1748). Physician. Friend of John Ray. The second son of a wealthy merchant from Yorkshire. Went up to St John's College in 1673. His first of many hundred letters to Ray appears to have been in 1681. Travelled in Europe to enhance his scholarship. Became a Secretary of the Royal Society for a brief period and subsequently, according to Raven, became the main link between John Ray and other scientists and exerted a significant influence within the scientific community. Known to have visited John Ray at Black Notley in May 1686. Highly valued by John who discussed all his plans with him as well as submitting the manuscripts of his books for his appraisal. Became physician to George I.

Rondelet, Guillaume. (1507-1566). From Montpellier. Studied medicine and anatomy in Paris. Said to have presided over the greatest school of Botany in Europe in the sixteenth century. Ray used his *De Piscibus Marinis*, published in Lyons in 1554, as one of his main authorities in his own work *Historia Piscium*.
Salviani, Hippolyto. (1514-1572). Physician to three successive popes. His publication *Aquatilium Animalium Historiae*, published in 1554 contained particularly fine plates and engravings of fishes, which John Ray copied.
Sloane, Hans. (1660-1753). Physician and naturalist. President of the Royal Society (1727-1740), succeeding Isaac Newton. Friend of John Ray. His large private collections of books, manuscripts and pictures prompted the founding of the British Museum. While in Jamaica he collected over 800 new plants.
Steno, Nicholas. (1638-1686) Danish anatomist and geologist. Demonstrated that fossils were the petrified remains of ancient living organisms. A major contributor to the scientific revolution of the 17th century. Originally a physician who discovered the duct of the parotid salivary gland. Later became a Roman Catholic bishop.
Swammerdam, Johannes (1637-1680) Dutch naturalist. Much of his work was involved in collecting and studying insects describing their anatomy and life histories and then dividing them into four groups. His *General History of Insects*, published in Utrecht in 1669, was used by John Ray who considered it "the best book that was ever written on that subject." Swammerdam used a microscope (invented in 1609 by the Dutch spectacle maker Zacharias Janssen) to make excellent pictures of his subjects.
Theophrastus, (c371-287BC) Greek philosopher and scientist who studied under Plato and who became Aristotle's greatest friend, succeeding him at the Academy. He is identified as establishing botany as a science. His work was preserved and developed by Muslim Scholars before being appreciated and studied in Europe some fifteen hundred years after his death.

Turner, William. (1508-1568) Herbalist. Said to have been John Ray's predecessor in natural history at Cambridge. A student at Pembroke Hall, elected to Fellowship in 1531. Travelled widely on the continent, partly because his religious beliefs did not find favour in England. Met Gesner and studied Botany at Bologna. His religious beliefs and enthusiasm for the Reformation led to a further period abroad where he published the second part of his *Herbal* in Cologne in 1562. The third part was also published in Cologne in 1568. Admired by John Ray for his sound learning and judgement.

White, Gilbert. (1720-1793) Naturalist. Following ordination in the Anglican Church in 1751 he began to make observations of the natural history surrounding his home. His collection of correspondence with other naturalists is admired in particular for his keen observation and descriptive style. He credited John Ray with similar qualities: "Ray is supreme in description, in the concise accounts he gives of....plants, birds, fishes and insects." Raven states that John Ray's *Wisdom of God manifested in the works of Creation* provided the background to Gilbert White's thoughts about the natural world.

Wilkins, John. (1614-1672). Master of Trinity College in 1659 but deposed after the 'Restoration.' Married to Oliver Cromwell's sister. Son of a goldsmith from Oxford. According to Raven, 'he derived from his father a love of intricate mechanism and a practical ingenuity which in that first age of applied science attracted him to men like Boyle and Hooke' and he ' had imagination of high order and courage both speculative and moral; energy to accomplish and stimulate hard work; and charm to enable him to survive the cataclysms of the time without compromising his opinions or ruining his career.' In 1668 became Bishop of Chester. According to Raven he had a significant encouraging influence upon John Ray who held him in admiration, their acquaintance beginning at Trinity and strengthened by virtue of Wilkins' friendship with Francis Willughby. First Secretary of the Royal Society.

Willughby, Emma. Wife of Francis Willughby. Following the death of Francis in 1672 she married Josiah Child. The reasons for her dislike of John Ray are not clear.

Willughby, Francis. (1635-1672). Perhaps John Ray's closest friend and professional colleague. The only son of Sir Francis and Cassandra Willughby of Middleton Hall, Warwickshire and Wollaton, Nottinghamshire. Was initially a pupil of John Ray at Trinity. Francis had a distinguished career in Cambridge especially in mathematics. Described as a man of delicate physique but 'remarkable beauty' with a charm of expression and 'of ardent and restless temperament, great ability and industry' (Raven). His health was never robust and it is possible that his wife blamed John Ray for encouraging her husband on their travels and expeditions, which would have been arduous and risky for his fragile health. John Ray is clear that it was Francis who fired his imagination and determination for them both to set out to make a systematic record of the whole of the natural world.

Wren, Christopher. (1632-1723) Architect and scientist having studied science and mathematics at Oxford. A founder member of the Royal Society and president 1680-82. Following the fire of London (1666) he was commissioned to rebuild 51 city churches and 36 company halls. His famous design for St Paul's was accepted in 1675 where he was buried in 1723.

Chronology

1625. James I dies and is succeeded by Charles I.
1627. 29th November. Birth of John Ray at Black Notley
6th December Christened at Black Notley church.
1636. Charles decrees that the Scottish Church should be ruled by bishops.
1638. The National Covenant in Scotland challenges the King's power.
Joseph Plume becomes Rector of Black Notley church.
John Ray commences at the Braintree 'Grammar School' in St Michael's Church.
1640. Parliament refuses funds requested by Charles.
1642. Charles tries to impeach five members of the House of Commons. Beginning of the Civil War.
1643. Alliance between Parliament and Scottish people
1644. June. John Ray enters Catherine Hall, Cambridge, at the age of 16.
1645. Archbishop Laud executed. Defeat of Charles who surrenders to the Scots
1646. November. John Ray transfers to Trinity College, Cambridge, now aged 18.
1647. Scots surrender Charles to Parliament. Army seizes Him.
1648. John Ray graduates as B.A., aged 20.
1649. Charles is tried for treason and executed.
Oliver Cromwell takes control of the country.
John Ray is elected a Minor Fellow at Cambridge.
1650, Charles II is crowned in Scotland
Start of illness of John Ray, now aged 22, requiring a prolonged period of convalescence leading to his starting to study botany.
1651. John Ray appointed Lecturer in Greek and obtains M.A. degree.
Cromwell defeats Charles II at Worcester and Charles escapes to France.
1653. Cromwell becomes Lord Protector.

John Ray appointed Mathematics Lecturer, now aged 25.
1655. Cromwell dissolves Parliament.
John Ray appointed Lecturer in Humanities.
1656. Start of the 3-year war with Spain
John Ray's father dies. He has Dewlands built for his mother.
1658. Oliver Cromwell dies, succeeded by his son Richard.
John Ray Journeys to Derbyshire and North Wales alone, aged 30. Appointed Junior Dean (Dean:Resident Fellow appointed to supervise conduct and studies of junior members of a College)
1659. Parliament quarrels with the Army and Richard Cromwell agrees to resign.
1660. Charles II becomes King.
John Ray's *Catalogus Cantabrigiam* published.
Journeys to Northern England and Isle of Man with Francis Willughby. On the 23rd December he is ordained.
1661. Journey to York, Edinburgh, Glasgow and Carlisle with Skippon.
1662. January: journey to Sussex. April: London and Cambridge where he completed his last botanising in that area. May:Journey round Wales with Willughby and Skippon; then to Lands End with Skippon.
24th August resigns his Fellowship because of the Act of Uniformity. Unable to practise either as a tutor or clergyman.
1663. Journey to Kent and then through the Low Countries, up the Rhine to Vienna and Venice. Now aged 35.
1664. Spends winter in Padua studying anatomy. In the spring at Genoa and Naples. In the Summer Sicily, Malta, Florence and Rome. While in Rome he studies birds and fishes in the markets.
1665. War between England and Netherlands.
Great Plague decimates the population of London by a third.
John Ray still on the continent at Venice and Geneva. Later at Montpellier. Now aged 37.
1666. Spring: travels from Montpellier to Paris, Calais and returns to Essex. June: Visits Cambridge and Sussex.
French declare war on England.

Great Fire of London 2nd to 5th September.
John Spends the winter at Middleton Hall with Willughby.
1667. Peace agreed between Dutch, French and English.
John Ray journeys to Worcester, Gloucester, Cornwall, Dorset, and Hants. In September he is back in Black Notley seriously ill.
In November he is admitted as a Fellow of the Royal Society.
1668. Charles II's brother, James, becomes a Roman Catholic.
John Ray, now 40, journeys to London, Essex, Yorkshire and Westmoreland. In September he is back at Middleton Hall, returning to Black Notley at the end of the month. He returns to Middleton Hall for November and December.
1669. January. In Chester with Wilkins. February-March: At Middleton Hall conducting experiments on sap. April: back at Chester where he dissects a porpoise. May; Back at Middleton then off again to Dorking, Oxford and Dartford.
1670. April: at Wollaton with Willughby. July at Middleton Hall. August: his *Catalogus Angliae* and *Collection of English Proverbs* are published.
1671. Spring: suffers from Jaundice at Middleton. June: visits Cambridge. July: Journeys to Settle, Berwick, and Brignall. Back at Middleton in the autumn and at the Royal Society in London in November. In December starts a two-month stay at Chester with Wilkins.
1672. England at war with the Dutch.
February-early March: John Ray at Middleton, followed by a visit to Black Notley then back to Middleton until November. Francis Willughby dies on the 3rd July.
November: in London. On the 19th Wilkins died and John returned to Middleton.
1673. Test Act excludes Catholics and Nonconformists from holding public office.
In February John Ray has *Observations and Catalogus Exteris* published. Marries Margaret Oakley on the 5th June at Middleton. Later that year his *Collection of English Words* is published.

1674. Peace is declared between England and the Dutch.
1675. Greenwich Observatory founded. Work begins on St Paul's Cathedral, London.
John Ray's *Dictionariolium* is published. Leaves Middleton Hall for Coleshill.
1676. Moves to Sutton Coldfield. In the summer visits Essex. Has Willughby's *Ornithologia* published..
1677. William of Orange marries Mary, daughter of James II. In September John Ray refuses the Secretaryship of the Royal Society. In November he and his wife leave Sutton Coldfield for Faulkbourne Hall, near Witham, Essex. Also the second edition of his *Catalogus Angliae* is published.
1678. John Ray has the English version of *Ornithologia* published as also the second edition of his *Collection of Proverbs*.
1679. Disabling Act bars Roman Catholics from entering Parliament. John Ray's Mother dies on the 15th March. In June he and his wife move to Dewlands. He is now 51 years old.
1682. Has *Methodus Plantarum* published.
1684. 12th August Birth of the Ray's twin daughters, Margaret and Mary. John is 56.
1685. Charles II dies, succeeded by his brother James II. Monmouth claims the throne. Hundreds of rebels hanged or sold as slave labour.
1686. James introduces pro-Catholic measures.
John Ray has Willughby's *Historia Piscium* Published and also the first volume of his *Historia Plantarum*.
1687. 3rd April Birth of their third daughter, Catherine. He is now 59.
1688. Has the second volume of *Historia Plantarum* Published. Also *Fasciculus Stirpium Britannicarum*.
1689. 10th February, birth of fourth daughter, Jane. He is now 61.
Son also born to James II. William of Orange invited to England by English Lords. James flees. Parliament declares that James has abdicated. Offers the throne to William and Mary.

Toleration Act, allowing dissenters and Roman Catholics freedom from the established church.

1690. William defeats James at the battle of the Boyne in Ireland and James makes his escape to France.

In March John Ray is ill with pneumonia. In May his *Synopsis Britannicarum* is published.

1691. Has *Wisdom of God manifested in the works of the Creation* published. Also the second edition of *Collection of English Words*.

1692. Has *Miscellaneous Discourses* published. Also the second edition of *Wisdom of God*.

1693. Has published Synopsis *Quadrupedum* and *Collection of Curious Travels* and three *Physico-Theological Discourses*.

1694. Death of Queen Mary. Bank of England founded.

John Ray has *Sylloge Europeanarum* published.

1696. Has *Dissertatio de Methodis* published. Also second edition of *Synopsis Britannicarum* and third edition of *Nomenclator Classicus*.

1698. Death of his daughter, Mary, on the 29th January. In July illness of his wife and daughter Margaret. John Ray is in his 71st year.

1700. Has published *Persuasive to a Holy Life*.

1701. Act of Settlement establishes Protestant Succession. Death of the exiled James II.

John Ray has third edition of *Wisdom of God* published.

1702. William III dies and is succeeded by his sister-in law, Anne. The first English Daily newspaper, the *Daily Courant*, is published.

1703. Work begins on the building of Buckingham Palace for the Duke of Buckingham. (To become a Royal residence in 1761).

John Ray has *Methodus Emendata* published as also the fourth edition of *Nomenclator Classicus*. Now aged 75.

1704. Gibraltar captured from Spain. In March John Ray seriosly ill. In August he has the third volume of *Historia Plantarum*, *Methodus Insectorum* and the fourth edition of *Wisdom of God,* published.

1705. 17th January: John Ray dies at Dewlands aged 77.
1707. Union of England and Scotland as Great Britain.
1710. St Paul's Cathedral finished. John Ray's *Historia Insectorum,* published.
1713. Publication of John Ray's *Synopsis Avium et Piscium* and the third edition of his *Physico-Theological Discourses.*
1714. Queen Anne dies. George I becomes King.

Sources

Baker, Michael. *The Book of Braintree and Bocking,* originally published in 1981, third edition in 2000.
Baldwin, Stuart. *John Ray Essex Naturalist, 1986,* published by Baldwin's Books.
Berry, R J. *John Ray father of Natural Historians,* prepared for the 1999 conference: John Ray and his successors, published in the conference papers by the John Ray Trust
Bragg, Melvyn, *The Adventure of English,* 2003, published by Hodder and Stoughton.
Briggs, Asa. *A Social History of England,* 1983, published by Book Club Associates.
Gribbin, John. *Science a History,* 2002, published by Penguin Books.
Crump, Thomas. *A Brief History of Science as seen through the development of Scientific instruments,* 2001, published by Constable and Robinson.
Cutler, Alan. *The Seashell on the Mountaintop,* 2004, published by Arrow Books.
Hedley Brooke, John. *'Wise Men Nowadays Think Otherwise*' prepared for the 1999 conference: John Ray and his successors. Published in the conference papers by the John Ray Trust.
Hunt, William. *The Puritan Movement.* 1983. Published by Harvard University Press.
John Ray Trust. *John Ray and his Successors,* 1999 Conference papers, edited by Nigel Cooper. Published by The John Ray Trust
Kenyon, J P, *Stuart England,* originally published 1978, reprinted by Penguin Books in 1990.
Keynes, Geoffrey. *The Bibliography of John Ray,* 1950/51 Faber and Faber.
Kingfisher Series. *Tudors and Stuarts,* 1997 edition. Editor James Harrison.
Kishlansky, Mark. *A Monarchy Transformed Britain 1603-1714,*1996, published by Allen Lane/The Penguin Press.

Ladybird Books, *The Stuarts,* 1994 edition in their History of Britain Series.
Lynch, Michael. *The Interregnum 1649-60, 1994,* Hodder and Stoughton.
McMahon, Susan. *'In these times of giddiness and distraction',* paper prepared for the 1999 conference: John Ray and his Successors published in the conference papers by the John Ray Trust. Also: *Constructing Natural History in England (1650-1700),* 2001, Thesis submitted to the University of Alberta.
Millar, John. *The Restoration and the England of Charles II, second edition 1987.* Seminar Studies in History. Published by Longman.
Morgan, Kenneth. *The Oxford History of Britain.* Published by Oxford University Press, updated edition, 2001.
Morrill, John. *Stuart Britain,* published in 1984 by Oxford University Press.
Neale, Kenneth. *Essex in History* published in 1997 by Philimore and Co Ltd.
Polkinghorne, John. *One World* the *interaction of science and theology,* Originally published 1986, sixth edition in 1990 by SPCK. Also *Science and Creation the search for understanding,* 1988, fourth impression 1990, also published by SPCK
Price, Colin. *John Ray's Wisdom of God in the dissenting tradition,* prepared for the 1999 conference: John Ray and his successors. Published in the conference papers by the John Ray Trust.
Raven, Charles. *John Ray Naturalist,* originally published in 1942, second edition 1950 and reissued in 1986 in the Cambridge Classics Series.
Ray, John, *The Wisdom of God manifested in the works of the Creation,* 1691.
Ray Society. *Memorials of John Ray,* Edited by Edwin Lankester, 1846.
Ray Society. *Further correspondence of John Ray,* Edited by Robert W. T Gunther, 1928.

Slack, Paul. *The impact of the Plague in Tudor and Stuart England,* 1985, published by Routledge & Kegan Paul.
Vardy, Peter. *The Puzzle of God,* 1999, published by Fount Paperbacks.